Shire County Guide 18

HERTFORDSHIRE

Arthur Jones

D0818727

Shire Publications Ltd

Printed in Great Britain by CIT Printing Services, Press Buildings, Merlins Bridge, Haverfordwest, Dyfed SA61 1XF.

British Library Cataloguing in Publication Data.
Jones, Arthur
  Hertfordshire. — 2 Rev. ed. — (Shire County Guides; No. 18).
  I. Title. II. Series.
  914. 25804
  ISBN 0-7478-0201-7

Cover: *Ashridge House.*

ACKNOWLEDGEMENTS
Photographs are acknowledged as follows: *Abbey News*, page 69; Cadbury Lamb, pages 11,14, 16, 17, 18, 21, 24, 25, 29, 31, 37, 38, 43, 45, 50, 51, 52, 66, 72, 78 (both), 81, 82, 84, 85, 88, 89, 90, 91, 92, 93, 94, 95, 96, 104, 105 and cover; the Marquess of Salisbury, page 75; the Natural History Museum, page 98; Three Rivers District Council, page 77; Verulamium Museum, pages 56, 97 (both); Watford Museum, page 99; Welwyn Roman Baths (photograph: Tony Rook), page 57. Other photographs are by the author.

Ordnance Survey grid references

Although information on how to reach most of the places described in this book by car is given in the text, National Grid References are also included in many instances, particularly for the harder-to-find places in chapters 3, 4 and 7. For the benefit of those readers who have the Ordnance Survey 1:50,000 Landranger maps of the area the references are stated as a Landranger sheet number followed by the 100 km National Grid square and the six-figure reference.

To locate a site by means of the grid reference, proceed as in the following example: The Aubreys (OS 166: TL 095113). Take the OS Landranger map sheet 166 ('Luton, Hertford and surrounding area'). The grid numbers are printed in blue around the edges of the map. (In more recently produced maps these numbers are repeated at 10 km intervals throughout the map, so that it is not necessary to open it out completely.) Read off these numbers from the left along the top edge of the map until you come to 09, denoting a vertical grid line, then estimate five-tenths of the distance to vertical line 10 and envisage an imaginary vertical grid line 09.5 at this point. Next look at the grid numbers at one side of the map (either side will do) and read *upwards* until you find the horizontal grid line 11. Estimate three-tenths of the distance to the next horizontal line above (i.e. 12), and so envisage an imaginary horizontal line across the map at 11.3. Follow this imaginary line across the map until it crosses the imaginary vertical line 09.5. At the intersection of these two lines you will find The Aubreys.

The Ordnance Survey Landranger maps which cover Hertfordshire are sheets 153, 154, 165, 166, 167 and 176.

Contents

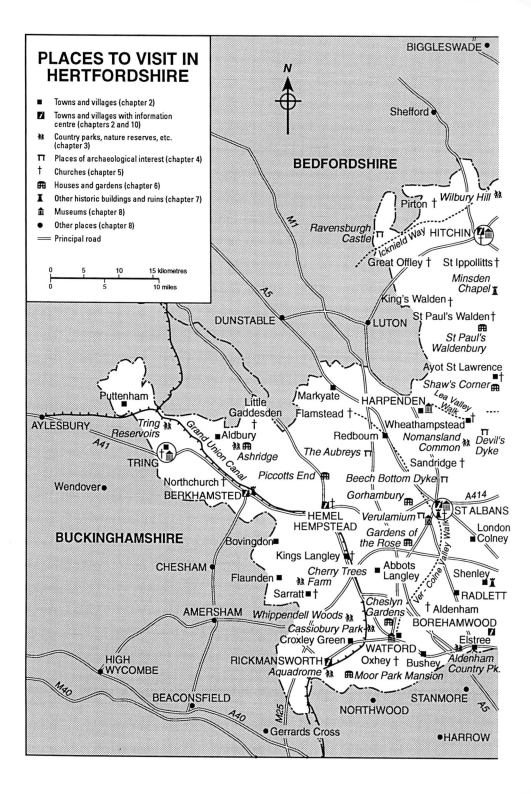

PLACES TO VISIT IN HERTFORDSHIRE

- ■ Towns and villages (chapter 2)
- ⅄ Towns and villages with information centre (chapters 2 and 10)
- ⅄⅄ Country parks, nature reserves, etc. (chapter 3)
- ⊓ Places of archaeological interest (chapter 4)
- † Churches (chapter 5)
- ⊞ Houses and gardens (chapter 6)
- Ⅰ Other historic buildings and ruins (chapter 7)
- 🏛 Museums (chapter 8)
- ● Other places (chapter 8)
- ═ Principal road

0 ___ 5 ___ 10 ___ 15 kilometres
0 ___ 5 ___ 10 miles

N

BIGGLESWADE ●

Shefford ●

BEDFORDSHIRE

M1

Pirton † Wilbury Hill ⅄⅄

Ravensburgh Castle ⊓ Icknield Way HITCHIN ⅄🏛

Great Offley † St Ippollitts †

Minsden Chapel Ⅰ

King's Walden †

St Paul's Walden †

St Paul's Waldenbury ⊞

DUNSTABLE ● LUTON

Ayot St Lawrence ■ †
Shaw's Corner ⊞

A5

Puttenham

Little Gaddesden

Markyate ■ HARPENDEN 🏛

Flamstead †

Lea Valley Walk

Wheathampstead †

AYLESBURY ●

Tring Reservoirs ⅄⅄

Aldbury ■

Redbourn ■

Nomansland Common ⅄⅄ Devil's Dyke ⊓

A41

Grand Union Canal

Ashridge ⅄⅄⊞

The Aubreys ⊓

Sandridge †

TRING 🏛

Wendover ●

Northchurch †

Piccotts End ⊞

Beech Bottom Dyke ⊓

BERKHAMSTED ⅄

Gorhambury ⊞

A414

BUCKINGHAMSHIRE

Ⅰ †

HEMEL HEMPSTEAD

Verulamium ⊓ 🏛 ST ALBANS ⅄🏛

London Colney ●

Bovingdon ■

Gardens of the Rose ⊞

Kings Langley ■ †

CHESHAM ●

Cherry Trees Farm ⅄⅄

Abbots Langley ■

Shenley ■

Flaunden ■

Cheslyn Gardens ⊞

† Aldenham

RADLETT Ⅰ

Sarratt ■ †

Ver-Colne Valley Walk

BOREHAMWOOD ⅄

AMERSHAM ●

Whippendell Woods ⅄⅄

Cassiobury Park ⅄⅄

Croxley Green ■

WATFORD 🏛

Oxhey †

Bushey ■

Elstree ⅄

Aldenham Country Pk. ⅄⅄

RICKMANSWORTH ⅄

Aquadrome ⅄⅄

Moor Park Mansion ⊞

HIGH WYCOMBE ●

M25

STANMORE ●

M40

BEACONSFIELD ●

A40

NORTHWOOD ●

A5

● Gerrards Cross

● HARROW

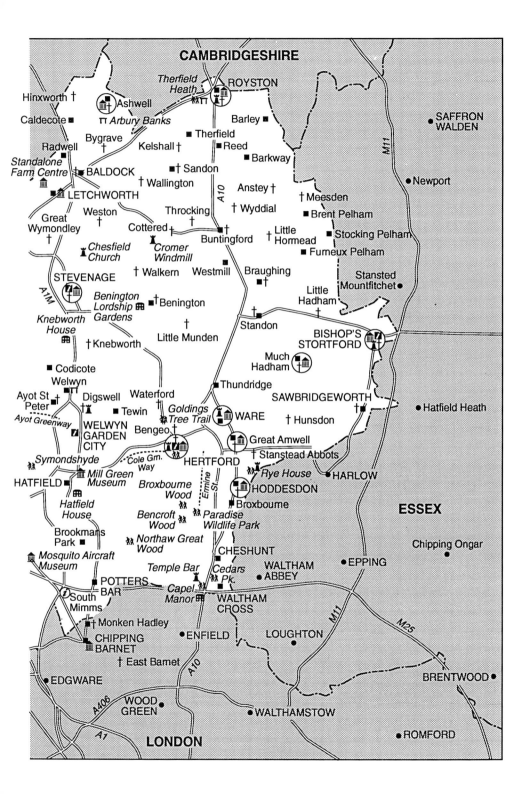

Preface

Welcome to the Shire County Guide to Hertfordshire, one of over thirty such books, written and designed to enable you to organise your time in each county well.

The Shire County Guides fill the need for a compact, accurate and thorough guide to each county so that visitors can plan a half-day excursion or a whole week's stay to best advantage. Residents, too, will find the guides a handy and reliable reference to the places of interest in their area.

Travelling British roads can be time consuming, and the County Guides will ensure that you need not inadvertently miss any interesting feature in a locality, that you do not accidentally bypass a new museum or an outstanding church, that you can find an attractive place to picnic, and that you will appreciate the history and the buildings of the towns or villages in which you stop.

This book has been arranged in special interest chapters, such as the countryside, historic houses or archaeological sites, and all these places of interest are located on the map on pages 4-5. Use the map either for an overview to decide which area has most to interest you, or to help you enjoy your immediate neighbourhood. Then refer to the nearest town or village in chapter 2 'Hertfordshire towns and villages' to see, at a glance, what special features or attractions each community contains or is near. The subsequent chapters enable readers with a particular interest to find immediately those places of importance to them, while the cross-referencing under 'Hertfordshire towns and villages' assists readers with wider tastes to select how best to spend their time.

1
The pattern of Hertfordshire

The administrative county of Hertfordshire was created in Saxon times. It was separated from the former county of Middlesex (now Greater London) in the south by a border which followed no natural feature, perhaps indicating an agreed line of partition taking account of the estate boundaries existing at the time. On the east the county is bounded by the rivers Lea and Stort, and on the north and north-west by the curve of the Chiltern Hills. Westward the county stretches out beyond Berkhamsted into Buckinghamshire, scooping up the town of Tring and the strategically important pass through the western Chilterns.

These county boundaries have been modified from time to time, most recently in 1965, when following the London Government Act of 1964 the Barnet peninsula became part of Greater London and Potters Bar was moved from the former county of Middlesex into Hertfordshire. (East Barnet, Chipping Barnet and Monken Hadley have nevertheless been included in this volume.)

Population has increased rapidly in the twentieth century, not only with the general increase in population but also through the establishment of Britain's first two 'garden cities', at Letchworth and Welwyn Garden City, and the development after the Second World War of three new towns at Stevenage, Hatfield and Hemel Hempstead. In 1901 the population of the county was 240,000; in 1951 it was 610,000; and in 1991 it was 989,000. In size of population Hertfordshire is now sixth among the 39 non-metropolitan counties in England, whereas in area (630 square miles or 1630 sq km) it is 34th.

Variety

In spite of this moderate size the variety of the terrain is remarkable. Along the southern border, from Rickmansworth and Bushey in the west to Potters Bar and Cheshunt in the east, many places have a suburban air and serve partly as dormitories for London: indeed, daily commuting to London, mainly by rail, is now common throughout the county. A further band, south of a line through Hemel Hempstead, St Albans and Hertford, lies within the Metropolitan Green Belt, which has afforded some protection for its mainly rural and agricultural character, and the county council has been concerned to extend similar protection to the wide rural areas elsewhere in the county. On the east the Lea and the Stort were formerly busy working rivers, but the wharves at Hertford, Ware, Sawbridgeworth and Bishop's Stortford are now mostly demolished or disused. Below Hoddesdon the Lea valley, formerly a major source of market-garden produce, notably tomatoes, for London, is now being developed as a recreational park.

The gently rolling centre of the county is characterised by a scatter of small towns and attractive villages, many of the latter extremely remote down narrow lanes. This is still a truly agricultural landscape consisting for the most part of working farms. City commuters and pensioners are certainly to be found, but they have come here to enjoy the quiet delights of the landscape and the great majority are careful not to spoil or overwhelm it. The Chiltern Hills, which fence in this landscape to the west and north, provide their own variety, from the heavy beechwoods, reminiscent of neighbouring Buckinghamshire, in the west to the close turf of chalk downs east of the Hitchin gap. Here, from the road which follows the ridge, there are great unobstructed views across Bedfordshire and Cambridgeshire to the north.

Structure

The key to the variety of the Hertfordshire landscape lies in its underlying geological structure. Hertfordshire lies on the northern rim of a saucer of chalk, which dips down below London and the Thames basin and re-emerges (its southern rim) as the North Downs. The middle of the saucer is filled with London clay, the material through which London's underground tunnels have been driven with such ease. This clay extends far enough to the north to cover a small part of Hertfordshire, up to a line from Watford to Bishop's Stortford. Chalk is close to the surface throughout most of the rest of the county, but in the north-east corner it was overridden by the glaciers of the last ice age which deposited a layer of chalky boulder clay and gravel, together with lumps of a conglomerate which has since aroused considerable curiosity under its popular name of Hertfordshire puddingstone. West and north of the Chilterns, notably around Tring and Ashwell, are areas of Gault clay which elsewhere underlies the chalk but reaches the surface at these points.

These varied geological patterns and the resulting soil types are reflected in the natural vegetation, the agriculture and even the industries of Hertfordshire. The alkaline soils in the north of the county account for the beechwoods and the rich flora of the Chil-

The Balloon Stone, Standon Green End.

terns. They also produce good yields of cereal crops, and the soils on the boulder clay of the north-east have proved particularly suitable for the cultivation of barley to meet the needs of the county's malting industry. It was as a result of the damage caused by heavily laden wagons of barley that in 1663 the road through Royston and Wadesmill to Ware was designated the first turnpike road in Britain, the cost of its upkeep being thereby transferred from parish rates to tolls paid by passing traffic. Rich deposits of gravel have been extracted from many sites around Hatfield and in the Lea valley.

Industries

Hertfordshire in 1838 had some eighty maltings, mostly in the north and east of the county. The industry declined after 1880 and only one is now in operation, but many of the impressive buildings survive (for example in Ware, Bishop's Stortford and Baldock) converted to other uses. Another industry, peculiar to north Hertfordshire and south Bedfordshire in the nineteenth century, and closely associated with agriculture, was straw plaiting. This 'cottage industry' was widespread throughout the area, where it involved probably the majority of working women and many children, and significantly reduced the incidence of poverty, and hence unrest.

The main industrial area in the county developed during the nineteenth century around the fast-growing town of Watford, which became a major centre for the printing industry. Hertfordshire has also made a significant contribution to the British film industry, with early experiments at St Albans, the main concentration of studios in Elstree and Borehamwood, and an offshoot during the 1930s at Welwyn Garden City. The county also has a place in the annals of aviation: the first balloon landing in Britain was made in 1784 by Lunardi at Standon Green End (see page 42); the first accident involving the death of airmen on active military service occurred during army manoeuvres on 6th September 1912, when Captain Hamilton and Lieutenant Wyness Stuart were killed while trying to make an emergency landing on a temporary airfield near Willian — they are commemorated by a memorial beside the country lane from Willian to Great Wymondley; during the First World War, on 3rd September 1916, there occurred the spectacular destruction of a German Zeppelin at Cuffley; and in the Second World War two military airfields, since dismantled, were built at Nuthampstead (see page 12) and Hunsdon, and the Mosquito bomber was manufactured in a garden at London Colney (see page 99). No commercial airfield exists in the county, but there have been five private fields, of which two are still in use: at Hatfield (De Havilland/Hawker Siddeley/British Aerospace) and Elstree.

The London factor

Proximity to London has influenced the development of Hertfordshire in two major respects. Throughout the centuries the county has been a favoured residence for courtiers, politicians and businessmen who needed a country home within easy reach of the capital: unlike the counties south of London it did not suffer in the early years from the barrier of the river Thames, it was more obviously salubrious than Middlesex and more easily accessible than either Buckinghamshire or Essex. Private parks and grand country houses proliferated and are still a common feature, many of them remaining in private hands.

Hertfordshire, too, lies athwart the main routes from London to the north, and many towns have developed to take advantage of this fact. Traffic along the main roads was sufficient even in medieval times to cause some communities to abandon their existing settlements and move down to the roadside for the sake of trade. Chipping Barnet was the first stage out of London for coaches and posting traffic on the Great North Road and the Holyhead Road, and its large number of inns bore witness to this fact. Its fortunes slumped after 1838 with the coming of the railway, which bypassed Chipping Barnet and created a new suburb round the station at New Barnet. Railway stations throughout Hertfordshire soon attracted colonies of commuters who travelled daily to London.

The essence of Hertfordshire

There is nothing imposing about Hertfordshire. Charles Lamb called it 'Hearty,

An old house at Meesden.

homely, loving Hertfordshire', and E. M. Forster, another resident, 'England at its quietest; England meditative'. There are no great rivers here, but the river Lea was fished by Isaak Walton; no mountains or dramatic landscapes (few eminences are more than 500 feet, 150 metres, above sea level); and no great cities (only six towns have populations larger than forty thousand). The charm of the county lies in its gentle landscape, its many fine houses, and above all in the beauty of its villages with their many timbered, thatched and often colour-washed buildings.

The character of this countryside is much appreciated by those who get to know it. 'You can scarcely walk a mile anywhere', said Sir William Beach Thomas, 'without acquiring some sense of the rich continuity of its history and its wholly English character.' And William Cobbett, who came only as a visitor, wrote: 'What that man ever invented under the name of pleasure grounds can equal these fields in Hertfordshire!'

2
Hertfordshire towns and villages

Abbots Langley

Abbots Langley parish is a strip of land about a mile wide, lying on the north-east side of the river Gade between Watford and Hemel Hempstead. This *lang leah*, or long clearing, was granted to the abbot of St Albans in the time of Edward the Confessor. On the landward side, the parish church was sited beside the village High Street, a byroad linking the two major towns.

In 1797 the Grand Junction Canal from Brentford reached Hemel Hempstead via the Gade valley, and a few years later a connection was made through to the industrial Midlands. This new highway for trade brought a measure of prosperity to those canalside communities in which wharves were established. Among these was Abbots Langley, where in 1811 John Dickinson purchased Nash Mills, which were to become Britain's foremost centre for papermaking. On the canalside nearby was later established the Ovaltine factory and the model dairy farm, now converted to residential use.

In the locality: Grand Union Canal, page 52; Kings Langley church, page 64.

Aldbury

This is a beautiful example of a classic village green, complete with pond, stocks and village shop, overlooked by timber-framed houses and with the parish church just round the corner. Stocks Road, the main village street, is somewhat gentrified, but the buildings of Town Farm still have a frontage on to the north end of the green and help to preserve a sense of reality. The feeling of being on a film set is not entirely fanciful: Aldbury sits on the doorstep of the British film industry, and the green is a familiar background for many films on cinema and television screens.

In the locality: Ashridge Estate, page 49; Grand Union Canal, page 52; churches at
Little Gaddesden, page 65; and Northchurch, page 66; Ashridge House, page 74.*

Aldenham

Aldenham Country Park, page 49; church of St John the Baptist, page 59.

Anstey

Church of St George, page 59.

Ashwell

At the time of Domesday Book Ashwell was one of Hertfordshire's five boroughs, apparently a place of some importance. Its status declined thereafter: although malting was a thriving industry here in the seventeenth century, the village's weekly market had been discontinued by 1792. Brewing continued in the village until the 1950s, but in recent years prosperity has depended increasingly on Ashwell's attractiveness as a residence for commuters to London and Cambridge.

Architecturally, Ashwell is a delight. No set itinerary can do justice to it and the following suggestions should be supplemented by wider exploration. The museum in Swan Street makes a good starting point. Mill Street opposite passes the parish church, near which are several handsome timber-framed cottages, and the Merchant Taylors School (1681), now a field studies centre. To the west of the museum is Gardiners Lane with its fine cob wall, thatched as a protection from the rain. In an easterly direction, Swan Street becomes Hodwell, at the bend of which is the old lock-up (page 83), built in 1800 with clunch blocks from the former chantry chapel in the churchyard. From here a path leads to the springs which gave Ashwell its name and its original focus.

At the T-junction the High Street leads back westward, passing on the north side Foresters Cottages (a fourteenth-century hall-house with later crosswings) and Plait Hall,

The former Merchant Taylors School in Ashwell.

where straw plaiting was taught in the early nineteenth century. On the south side is a house dated 1681, heavily decorated with ornamental plasterwork (pargeting), and next to it the long sixteenth-century guildhouse of the Brotherhood of St John the Baptist. Further west along the High Street are Bear House (about 1480, formerly the Bear Inn) and Chantry House (sixteenth century). At the extreme west end of the village opposite the junction of roads to Hinxworth and Newnham a bridleway up Partridge Hill leads to the earthwork of Arbury Banks.

Church of St Mary, page 59: **Ashwell Village Museum**, page 87.

In the locality: Icknield Way, page 53; Arbury Banks, page 55; churches at Baldock, page 60; Bygrave, page 61; and Hinxworth, page 63.

The Ayots

Ayot St Lawrence and Ayot St Peter lie in wooded country west of Welwyn. Roads connecting Welwyn with Wheathampstead, Harpenden and Kimpton encircle them at a distance of 1 mile (1.6 km) or so, leaving them remote and undisturbed. The origin of the name 'Ayot' is uncertain, but if it derives from a word meaning 'island' it could only be a metaphorical reference to this isolation in woodland clearings. The main points of interest in the two villages are their remarkable churches and the former home of George Bernard Shaw, Shaw's Corner. The village street of Ayot St Lawrence is modest but attractive.

Ayot Greenway, page 50; old and new **churches of St Lawrence**, page 59; **church of St Peter**, page 60; **Shaw's Corner**, pages 78 and 106.

Baldock
Early closing, Thursday; market day, Wednesday.

Baldock was a considerable settlement in the iron age and in Roman times but was appar-

Church Street, Baldock, from the church tower.

ently abandoned in the fifth century. It lay east of the present High Street, between the roads to Royston and Wallington. During the 1980s that part of the site east of the Clothall road (A507) was covered by a housing estate. Until then the area was known as Wall Field, suggesting that some traces of Roman occupation still remained when the next settlers arrived.

The land on which the medieval town of Baldock was built had lain within the manor of Weston. It was granted about 1250 to the Knights Templar, who established here a borough and parish which they called Baldock, taking the name, it is believed, from the Old French name for Baghdad.

Baldock became a market town with a wide main street along which in later years the Great North Road traffic passed on its way northward from Stevenage. The parish church stands at the end of this street, in the oldest part of the medieval town. Modern Baldock preserved until recently two very impressive former industrial buildings: a disused malting beside the Royston road just east of the town (destroyed by fire in 1992), and the hosiery factory of the 1920s, briefly a film studio,

which is now Tesco's supermarket at the south end of the town.

Church of St Mary, page 60.

In the locality: Arbury Banks, page 55; churches at Ashwell, page 59 ; Bygrave, page 61; Cottered, page 61; Hinxworth, page 63; Kelshall, page 64; Sandon, page 70; Wallington, page 72; and Weston, page 73; Cromer Windmill, page 79; Ashwell Village Museum, page 87.

Barkway

Barkway has an elegant High Street which was at one time the turnpike road to Cambridge. It contains an astonishing variety of both timber-framed and brick houses of high quality. Nevertheless a main feature is the milestone just north of Barkway House. This is the most southerly, and most ornate, of fifteen erected by Trinity College, Cambridge, along the road between Cambridge and Barkway, which is the road to London. There are three others between Barkway and the county boundary north of Barley. The cast iron plates on these milestones were apparently added in the nineteenth century.

Nuthampstead was the site of a major

operational airfield during the Second World War. It lay mainly in Barkway parish but extended as far as the villages of Anstey and Meesden. During 1944-5 this was the base of 378th Heavy Bombardment Group of the United States Air Force, operating Flying Fortress bombers. A memorial now stands outside the Woodman public house (OS 154: TL 412346) beside the road from Anstey to Nuthampstead and close to the centre of the former airfield.

In the locality: churches at Anstey, page 59; Buntingford, page 61; and Wyddial, page 73.

Barley

This unpretentious village on what is now the back road to Cambridge is pleasant to wander around and has some very special features. One which provides a dramatic greeting to the traveller from the south is the gallows-type sign of the Fox and Hounds, which bridges Church End, the road to Saffron Walden. It was transferred to this public house, once the Waggon and Horses, in 1955 after the former Fox and Hounds, 150 yards (136 metres) to the north, had burned down. To the right of the sign there stands the small rectangular village cage (page 83). Farther along Church End, opposite the church (mostly 1871), is Barley's main treasure, its early Tudor 'town house' or village hall, restored about 1970.

In the locality: Anstey church, page 59.

Barnet

See under Chipping Barnet, page 22.

Belsize

Cherry Trees Farm, page 51.

Bengeo

Hertford Nature Walk, page 52; church of St Leonard, page 60.

Benington

At the centre is a picture-book village green, surrounded by beautifully kept cottages, many with exposed timbers. The church is on one side, and at the corner the entrance to Benington Lordship Gardens.

Church of St Peter, page 60; **Benington Lordship Gardens**, page 74.

In the locality: churches at Little Munden, page 65; and Walkern, page 72.

Berkhamsted

Early closing, Wednesday; market day, Saturday.

The Roman Akeman Street follows the valley of the river Bulbourne through a gap in the Chiltern Hills in a north-westerly direction. Later the Grand Union Canal and the London & Birmingham Railway followed the same route, all passing through Berkhamsted. Continuous settlement here has been traced only from the late Saxon period, when the earliest site was at Northchurch. After the Battle of Hastings it was at Berkhamsted that William of Normandy accepted the submission of London, going on to be crowned at Westminster. The building of the Norman castle close to the river must have begun soon afterwards: Domesday Book records the presence here of a *fessarius* (moat engineer?) and of 52 burgesses, which places Berkhamsted among Hertfordshire's five boroughs at that date.

A separate parish seems to have been created by about 1100, but the church, dedicated

The Trinity College milestone at Barkway.

Dean Incent's House (left) and Castle Street (right) in Berkhamsted.

to St James, has not survived. St Peter's, the present parish church, was built in the thirteenth century, east of the already existing market. The main area of the original town lay between St Peter's and the castle, including Castle Street and Mill Street, but later development has been mainly along the High Street. In the market area this had that common feature of medieval towns, a 'middle row' and a narrow 'back street' where former market stalls were gradually replaced by more permanent structures. At the western end of Middle Row there stood a Tudor market house of a common style with open arcades beneath to provide shelter for traders. It was destroyed in 1854.

Buildings of note now existing in Berkhamsted include Berkhamsted School immediately north of the church, which incorporates the 1544 grammar school founded by Dean John Incent. His jettied house is in the High Street opposite the church. There are some attractive houses in Castle Street and on the south side of the High Street. Westward from Dean Incent's house are the Swan Inn (about 1600) and the Sayer Almshouses (1684). On the north side is the old

town hall (1859), a Victorian Gothic building of considerable charm, now converted to an arcade of small shops.

Grand Union Canal, page 52; **Berkhamsted Castle**, page 79.

In the locality: Ashridge Estate, page 49; churches at Little Gaddesden, page 65; and Northchurch, page 66; Ashridge House, page 74.

Bishop's Stortford
Early closing, Wednesday; market day, Thursday.

During the eighteenth century, Bishop's Stortford became prosperous as a market centre for a large rural area, and a coaching town on the road between London and Norwich. Two major industries developed, malting and brewing, assisted from 1769 by improved water transport offered by the Stort Navigation. Several maltings survive, converted to other uses. This is a small town, thrust forward into Essex and obliged to assume a big-town role because there is no other candidate. It lies at a crossroads: the old road from Hadham to Dunmow (A1250) runs west to east through the town (through traffic now follows a bypass), and the road from London to Newmarket and Norwich runs south to north. Each of these roads follows an erratic course, and orientation in the town is difficult.

The natural town centre, the market square, is situated at an earlier crossroads within the present south-west quadrant. It is in this vicinity that the main buildings of interest are to be found, although Waytemore Castle mound lies just outside this quadrant, across the A1250. As befits an important coaching town, picturesque inns abound, many of them with interesting historical associations. What remains of the market place is now dominated by the grand neo-classical Corn Exchange (built 1828, restored and converted to shops and offices in 1974-5), which occupies half its original area. The town's four main streets (North Street, South Street, Main Street and Bridge Street) all lead out of the Market Place. The Corn Exchange looks down North Street towards the Chantry, in the fifteenth century probably the house of the chantry priest, but the present much grander building is mainly of the eighteenth century.

Water Lane, to the right at the bottom of North Street, describes an arc back to Bridge Street. It would once have skirted the water meadow which lies between here and the river Stort. In the seventeenth century this was the town's tannery quarter. Here now is the United Reformed Church (1860), overbearing in its bulk but with a truly impressive interior, including two galleries and extensive use of cast iron.

Facing Bridge Street beyond the Corn Exchange is High Street, where Tissiman's shop on the corner of Basbow Lane is the most conspicuous of several timber-framed buildings. Here also are some of the town's most notable inns. On the south side of the High Street is St Michael's parish church. At this point the street widens and becomes Windhill, where fairs and other festivities were customarily held. Windhill today is a street of elegant residences, many of them of the early nineteenth century. Next to St Michael's churchyard, in the former Windhill House, was until recently the Roman Catholic St Joseph's Monastery. Within the grounds is the church of St Joseph, whose windows contain some stained glass attributed to Albrecht Dürer.

Church of St Michael, page 61; **Waytemore Castle**, page 86; **Local History Museum**, page 87; **Rhodes Memorial Museum and Commonwealth Centre**, page 87.

In the locality: churches at Braughing, page 61; Little Hadham, page 65; Much Hadham, page 65; Sawbridgeworth, page 71; Forge Museum and Victorian Cottage Garden, page 94.

Borehamwood
See under Elstree, page 23.

Bovingdon and Flaunden
These two villages lie near the Buckinghamshire border, 2-4 miles (3-6 km) south-west of Hemel Hempstead. Until the middle of the nineteenth century they were not separate parishes but perpetual curacies served irregularly from Hemel Hempstead. The parishes contain some fine medieval hall-houses and cottages, including two of cruck construction in Church Lane, Bovingdon. Oak Cottage in Flaunden demonstrates clearly (and authentically) the practice of raising the height of the wall to increase headroom in an upper floor when the insertion of a chimney made two floors possible.

Bovingdon's church, which dates only from 1845, contains a notable effigy of a knight in armour of about 1400. Flaunden's medieval chapel lay in a remote spot over a mile (1.5 km) south of the village in the bend of the river Chess. It was built on a Greek cross plan, with four equal arms, and a curate's house attached. It was abandoned in 1838 when a new church was built in the village: any remains are now completely overgrown (OS 166: TQ 008987).

In the locality: Cherry Trees Farm, page 51.

Braughing
Braughing was a Roman town of some importance at the junction of Ermine Street (London-Ware-Lincoln) with roads serving St Albans, Colchester and Baldock. Its centre lay to the west of the present B1368 (Puckeridge-Barkway) road where it crosses the river Rib. Characteristically the Saxons

Gobions Folly Arch, Brookmans Park.

north side. It was along this path, in the sixteenth century, that the coffin of Matthew Wall was being carried to the churchyard for burial, when one of the bearers stumbled, causing it to fall. The jolt revived the still living occupant, who shortly afterwards passed the same way to his wedding! When he eventually died in 1595 his will provided for the annual sweeping of Fleece Lane, still performed on 2nd October each year.

Return down the lane to the church and follow The Causeway past the old Boys School (timber-framed with brick nogging) towards the ford, and so back along The Street to The Square. At the far end of The Street a road to the left returns to the B1368 by way of another ford.

Church of St Mary, page 61.

In the locality: churches at Buntingford, page 61; Little Hormead, page 65; and Standon, page 71.

Brookmans Park

Brookmans was one of two main medieval manors which, together with the small manor of More Hall or Gobions, made up the parish of North Mymms. Samuel Robert Gaussen purchased Brookmans in 1786 and it remained in the Gaussen family until 1923. The Gobions estate was added in 1838, and the two together now constitute the area known as Brookmans Park.

Both the former manor houses have been destroyed: More Hall, the medieval house at Gobions (once the property of Sir Thomas More), was replaced in the eighteenth century by an impressive new mansion which was itself demolished by Robert William Gaussen when he purchased the property in 1838. The seventeenth-century mansion at Brookmans was burnt down in 1891: until the estate was sold in 1923 the refurbished stable block served as the family residence, then the house was divided into five flats and later converted into the golf clubhouse. The conversion of Brookmans Park to a very attractive residential area, mainly for London commuters, was assisted in 1926 by the provision of a railway station at the west side of Brookmans Park on the line between Potters Bar and Hatfield. At

left this site undisturbed and established their own settlement (the present village) ½ mile (800 metres) farther north. Road access to the village from the south is now by a right turn at the war memorial on B1368 but, unless the river is exceptionally high, the more attractive and traditional route runs from Green End, 500 yards (460 metres) farther north, down Maltings Lane and across the ford. Then follow The Street to the left: it is possible to park by the pump in The Square.

This is one of the most handsome of Hertfordshire villages, with some fine examples of vernacular building. From the back of The Square the right-hand path leads through a gate into the churchyard for a good view of St Mary's church. After viewing the church pass out by the main gate: some of the finest houses face the churchyard on your right. Straight ahead is Fleece Lane, a footpath leading to Green End and the Golden Fleece public house. Notice Braughing chapel on the

(Opposite) The village stocks and pond at Aldbury.

the other end of the estate, on the east side of the old Great North Road (A1000), a BBC radio transmitter was established in 1929.

A curious relic of Gobions is the Folly Arch which survives in Hawkshead Road (OS 166: TL 254050). This sham medieval gateway was built about 1754 by Sir Jeremy Sambrooke (who also erected the battle of Barnet memorial at Monken Hadley). The arch originally formed the entrance to an avenue of trees leading to 'pleasure grounds', which included a lake, a woodland temple and a bowling green. Only the arch and the lake now remain.

In the locality: Northaw Great Wood, page 53.

Broxbourne

Broxbourne originated as a settlement beside the river Lea which became a Saxon estate and a Norman manor, with a mill which survived until 1949. (Its remains can still be seen at the bottom of Mill Lane.) There was a

The Seth Ward almshouses at Buntingford.

church here by 1086, probably near the Spitalbrook, where ruins were recorded in 1517. The present building dating from the fifteenth and sixteenth centuries contains the tomb of Sir John Say (died 1474) and his wife Lady Elizabeth, with their beautiful and much reproduced brasses.

The later development of Broxbourne has resulted from its location on three main transport routes: in the thirteenth century the Roman Ermine Street was largely abandoned in favour of a more easterly route between London and Ware following the valley of the river; the river itself, which had been a highway from earliest times, was subject to various 'improvements', particularly during the eighteenth century, to facilitate the carriage of goods as far as Ware; and in 1840 the Northern and Eastern Railway, subsequently the Great Eastern, also adopted a riverside route for its line between Shoreditch and Bishop's Stortford, with a station at Broxbourne. The area between the station and the main road was soon colonised by London commuters.

Southward, the vicinity of the parish church, enhanced by the New River from Great Amwell crossing its meadow, has remained delightfully unspoilt. Mill Lane, near the church, gives access to Broxbourne Meadows, with riverside walks in the Lea Valley Regional Park. There is ample accommodation for cars at the bottom of Mill Lane.

In the locality: Bencroft Wood, page 50; Broxbourne Wood, page 50; Paradise Wildlife Park, page 53; Ermine Street, page 56. See also under Hoddesdon, page 31; and Cheshunt, page 19.

Buntingford

Early closing, Wednesday; market day, Monday.

Buntingford grew up where Ermine Street crossed the river Rib. Four parishes meet in the vicinity: Layston, Throcking, Aspenden and Wyddial. From the thirteenth century onward the town developed gradually by attracting population from these parishes to serve the needs of travellers along the road. An existing market in Chipping, about 1 mile (1.6 km) to the north, was transferred into the town in 1360. Development has taken place mainly along the road north of the bridge, and within the curve of the river Rib. The High Street has some distinguished buildings spanning the sixteenth to nineteenth centuries, notably the Seth Ward almshouses of 1684. Round the corner south of the bridge the former union workhouse survives from the 1830s. The A10 road continued to pass through the town until the spring of 1987, when a bypass opened to through traffic.

Church of St Peter, page 61.

In the locality: churches at Anstey, page 59; Braughing, page 61; Cottered, page 61; Little Hormead, page 65; Meesden, page 65; Standon, page 71; Throcking, page 72; and Wyddial, page 73; Cromer Windmill, page 79.

Bushey
Early closing, Wednesday.

The village of Bushey grew around the parish church (St James), behind the village green and pond, and extends along the High Street. The still pleasantly rural character of this street is enhanced by the association of Bushey with Sir Hubert von Herkomer (died 1914) and the studios and school of art which he established here. The site of the school is now occupied by the southern part of 'The Rose Garden' in the High Street. Other buildings were located in and around Melbourne Road, farther to the east. Here on the left is the lonely remaining portion of Lulualand ('Herkomer's Castle') which now provides a noble entrance to the British Legion hall.

The late nineteenth-century development of Bushey can be seen reflected in the parish church. Compare the present spacious building with the narrow aisleless church which existed before 1870 (there is a photograph in the admirable church guide). The chancel of this long-standing church was built in the thirteenth century, the nave and tower some two hundred years later. There must have been an even earlier church in Bushey: a tablet in the tower makes dubious claim to an origin in 1006. The last great restoration and enlargement took place in 1870 when the addition of north and south aisles more than doubled the floor area. The church contains some interesting and unusual features. Three bays of blank arcading with Purbeck marble

shafts line each side of the chancel. Instead of a chancel arch, a tie beam in the fifteenth-century roof supports a lath and plaster tympanum bearing the royal arms of Queen Anne. There is a magnificent Jacobean pulpit, similar to that at Kings Langley, panelled, carved and retaining its original tester.

In the locality: Aldenham Country Park, page 49; Aldenham church, page 59; Oxhey Chapel, page 66. See also under Watford, page 46.

Bygrave
Church of St Margaret, page 61.

Caldecote
Caldecote is a deserted medieval village: the parish of only 325 acres (132 hectares) was one of the smallest in the county. Extensive excavation of the area has revealed evidence of prehistoric settlement with continuous occupation from about 1050. The site was largely abandoned during the fifteenth and sixteenth centuries. The only substantial buildings which remain are the manor house and the miniature but ambitiously designed church of St Mary Magdalene. This church, built about 1400, is now disused and in the care of the Friends of Friendless Churches. It is reasonably weathertight but shows inevitable signs of dilapidation. The only notable feature is the canopied water stoup in the south porch.

In the locality: churches at Ashwell, page 59; Hinxworth, page 63; Ashwell Village Museum, page 87.

Cheshunt
Early closing, Thursday.

Cheshunt parish church and the old village lie nearly a mile (1.6 km) to the west of the present busy High Street. The Roman Ermine Street, whose route passes close by the church, fell out of use here at an early date, and the town developed along a later road from London which followed the Lea valley to the river crossing at Ware. The modern A10 has returned some way towards the original alignment. The southern part of Cheshunt became the separate parish of Waltham Cross (see page 45) in 1855 and the southwestern part became the parish of Goff's Oak

Braughing village and St Mary's church.

(Opposite) The entrance to the municipal gardens by St Mary's church, Hemel Hempstead.

in 1871.

The fifteenth-century parish church of St Mary in the old village has few features of distinction although the parish alms chest is a particularly fine example dating from the seventeenth century. The cul-de-sac leading to Churchfields Path, opposite the church gate, retains its village character. Bishop's College in Churchgate was used first by the Countess of Huntingdon's Connection (1792-1905) and subsequently by the Church of England till 1968. The buildings, with striking modern additions, are now the offices of Broxbourne Borough Council.

In 1564 Elizabeth I's chief minister, Lord Burghley, built here his great house, Theobalds, which so took the fancy of James I that he persuaded Burghley's son Robert Cecil to exchange it for his palace at Hatfield (page 75). The house was demolished, mainly during the Commonwealth. The site on the south side of Theobalds Lane, east of the present Great Cambridge Road, was more recently occupied by The Cedars, now a public park, and Old Palace House, both destroyed during the twentieth century. Some fragments of Theobalds survive in the gardens of the park.

Cedars Park, page 51; **Temple Bar**, page 86.

In the locality: Bencroft Wood, page 50; Broxbourne Wood, page 50; Capel Manor Educational Farm, page 50; Northaw Great Wood, page 53; Capel Manor Gardens, page 74. See also Waltham Cross, page 45; Broxbourne, page 18; and Hoddesdon, page 31.

Chipping Barnet
Early closing, Thursday; market days, Wednesday and Saturday.

Barnet came into prominence as the first staging post for coaches using the Great North Road and the Holyhead Road out of London. It has a long uphill High Street dominated by the church adjoining the former market place. At this point Wood Street branches to the west, past Tudor Hall (1573), first home of the Queen Elizabeth Grammar School, the museum and some pleasant cottages. In Wellhouse Lane was formerly the union workhouse (partly surviving in Barnet General

Hospital) and in Well Approach the supposed 'physic well', whose water made Samuel Pepys ill in 1664, which has now been enclosed.

Beyond the church the Great North Road goes ahead to the site of the battle of Barnet, marked by Hadley Highstone. Before this is reached the A1081 (the former Holyhead Road) turns left towards South Mimms and St Albans, but this was an 1828 improvement: before that the road to Holyhead took a left fork behind Hadley Highstone.

Chipping Barnet church was formerly a chapel-of-ease of East Barnet. They were formally created two separate parishes in 1866. The church, which seems to have been rebuilt in the fifteenth century, was greatly enlarged in 1872. The nave and north aisle survive from the earlier building and there are good Ravenscroft monuments from the seventeenth century.

The long-surviving Barnet Horse Fair is still held every September, now in Mays Lane.

Barnet Museum, page 87.

In the locality: churches at East Barnet, page 62; and Monken Hadley, page 65. See also Monken Hadley, page 35.

Chiswell Green
The Gardens of the Rose, page 74.

Codicote
Codicote was a settlement on the road between Welwyn and Hitchin. The Great North Road passed through Knebworth farther to the east, but this was still quite a busy road linking London with Bedford and the east Midlands. The George and Dragon inn (now a restaurant called 'As You Like It') is the oldest recorded licensed house in the county: it has served travellers on this road since the thirteenth century. It became an important coaching inn, and many more inns grew up along the High Street, some still surviving. The road was turnpiked in 1763.

Codicote has its share of handsome houses, especially in the centre (note the eighteenth-century Pond House and Tithe Farm) where the open space opposite the George and Dragon accommodated the weekly market and an annual fair. The church stands close to the bury (or manor), a little apart from the

Evidence of the 'resurrection men', or body snatchers, in Codicote churchyard.

village, which is a not uncommon arrangement. A mile (1.6 km) along the road to
Hitchin is a remarkable house, built in 1927
as the Node Dairy and Stud, incorporating
perhaps the largest area of thatched roof in
the county.

*In the locality: churches at Ayot St Law-
rence, page 59; Knebworth, page 64; and St
Paul's Walden, page 70; Knebworth House
and Country Park, page 76; St Paul's Waldenbury, page 77; Shaw's Corner, page 78.*

Cottered
Church of St John the Baptist, page 61.

Cromer
Cromer Windmill, page 79.

Croxley Green
Croxley Green, within the present-day district of Three Rivers, extends from the river
Chess in the west to the Gade in the east, with
the Colne at its southern edge. The Saxon
estate which later became the manor of
Croxley was supposedly given to the abbot of
St Albans by King Offa. It remained the
property of the abbots until the dissolution of
the monastery in 1539, after which it was
acquired by John Caius. In 1557 he established Gonville and Caius College, Cam-

bridge, and gave this manor as an endow-
ment. The college remained in possession
until 1973, when the property was sold. Its
greatest treasure, the pre-Reformation tithe
barn, was acquired by Hertfordshire County
Council and restored in 1975. It stands on
private land but can be viewed from the public footpath (OS 166: TQ 072945). The
nearby manor house is of the sixteenth century. Some old cottages face on to the triangular green.

*In the locality: Grand Union Canal, page
52; Whippendell Woods, page 54; Sarratt
church, page 40. See also Watford, page 46;
and Rickmansworth, page 37.*

Digswell
Church of St John the Baptist, page 61;
Digswell Viaduct, page 80.

East Barnet
Church of St Mary the Virgin, page 62.

Elstree and Borehamwood
Elstree grew up along the road between London and St Albans (Watling Street) at the
point where it is crossed by the road from
Barnet to Bushey. (This road is now the
boundary between Hertfordshire and Greater
London.) The parish church (St Nicholas),

St Mary's church, Hitchin.

(Opposite) St Mary's church, Puttenham.

which lies just north of this junction, was rebuilt in 1853. Elstree parish extends 2 miles (3 km) eastward as far as the railway. Borehamwood became an independent parish in 1909, embracing the former hamlet of Borehamwood. This hamlet became established initially around the junction of Theobald Street and Shenley Road. To the north and south of the parish is a large concentration of postwar housing.

Elstree and Borehamwood both lie in the borough of Hertsmere and share a railway station midway between the two original settlements. Both are associated with the film industry, but only two studios remain, both flanking Shenley Road east of the station.

In the locality: Aldenham Country Park, page 49; Shenley Village Cage, page 86.

Flamstead
Church of St Leonard, page 62.

Graveley
Chesfield church (ruined), page 79.

Great Amwell
One of the most beautiful spots in Hertfordshire lies immediately below the parish church of Great Amwell, where in 1800 an island in the New River was laid out by Robert Mylne, architect to the New River Company, to commemorate the achievement of Sir Hugh Myddleton in creating the 'river' during the period 1609-13. The New River was an artificial channel which conveyed fresh water from Chadwell and other springs in this vicinity via Hoddesdon, Cheshunt, Hornsey and Holloway to a reservoir (the New River Head) in Clerkenwell. From there the water was distributed, originally by wooden pipes, throughout the north of London. Nineteenth-century pumping stations of quality and dignity occur at intervals along the Hertfordshire section.

2 miles (3 km) south of Great Amwell church, beyond the roundabout at St Margaret's, a road on the west side passes the impressive buildings of Haileybury College on its way to Hertford Heath. The college, established in 1809 as a training school for the East India Company, continued as a school when the company was wound up in 1857.

The buildings are not open to the public but inevitably excite interest. The architect was 27-year-old William Wilkins, whose later and best-known building, the National Gallery in Trafalgar Square, echoes many of the features of Haileybury.

Church of St John the Baptist, page 62; **Museum of Street Lighting**, page 87.

In the locality: churches at Hoddesdon, page 63; Hunsdon, page 63; Stanstead Abbots, page 71. See also Hoddesdon, page 31; and Ware, page 46.

Great Offley
Church of St Mary Magdalene, Offley, page 66.

Great Wymondley
Church of St Mary, page 62.

Harpenden
The handsome common on its south side is Harpenden's most attractive feature. Beyond it to left and right are prettified cottages and a hinterland of domestic splendour reminiscent of Surrey at its most opulent. At Hatching Green on the west side of the common, north of the road to Redbourn, stands Rothamsted Manor, a mainly seventeenth-century building of some grandeur with two pairs of Dutch gables on its south front. Much of the surrounding park is now public open space. The house is now a hall of residence for the adjoining Experimental Station for Agricultural Research, which grew from the work of Sir John Bennett Lawes (1814-1900), penultimate owner of the manor.

The laboratories which front the road are marked by a commemorative stone, mounted in front of the earlier laboratory building in 1893 — the fiftieth anniversary of the first of Rothamsted's agricultural experiments.

Southdown Road, east of the common, is crossed by the railway to London on a skew bridge which is a notable piece of railway architecture. Northwards along Southdown Road are the Moat House Hotel (mostly late eighteenth-century) and Harpenden Hall (partly sixteenth-century) which accommodates the Local History Centre. The main road (A1081) passes through Harpenden, with attractive leafy verges.

Harpenden Local History Centre, page 90; **Harpenden Railway Museum**, page 90.

In the locality: Lea Valley Walk, page 53; Nomansland Common, page 53; Devil's Dyke, page 56; churches at Flamstead, page 62; Sandridge, page 71; and Wheathampstead, page 73.

Hatfield

Early closing, Thursday; market days, Wednesday and Saturday.

Old Hatfield lies entirely on the east side of the railway, which arrived here in 1850. Since 1950 it has been complemented by Hatfield New Town, mainly west of the railway. The old town centre is only a few minutes walk from the railway station; motorists can usually find space in the car park opposite.

Hatfield grew up around the gateway of the palace of the Abbots and Bishops of Ely, now the site of Hatfield House at the top of Fore Street. Here, immediately outside the palace, stands Hatfield's parish church, dedicated to St Etheldreda, East Anglian princess and first abbess of Ely in the seventh century. The part of the church which is of greatest interest is the Salisbury Chapel, which contains Cecil family monuments and notable memorials to a thirteenth-century knight and to William Curll (died 1617). There is a Burne-Jones window in the south transept.

A good starting point for a walk round old Hatfield is the Eight Bells public house at the bottom of Fore Street, known for its Dickens associations (see page 102). Stroll up Georgian Fore Street, surely one of the most gracious streets in the county. Cross through the churchyard to Church Street and back down the hill towards the Eight Bells. At the bend in the road a flight of steps leads steeply down to the London Road. Until about 1970 at the foot of these steps was the former Salisbury Square which during the late nineteenth century had accommodated the staff of the Hertfordshire Militia. At the foot of the hill can be seen Marychurch, the circular Roman Catholic church opened in 1970. Its stained glass is particularly beautiful.

Proposals for a Victorian 'Hatfield New Town' were advertised in 1848, and some development did take place from that time in the vicinity of the present new town centre.

The opening of the 'Barnet Bypass' (A1) in 1927, and the building of De Havilland's factory (now British Aerospace) in the early 1930s stimulated development at the north end of the town. Then in 1948 Hatfield was designated as one of the postwar 'new towns', and rapid expansion continued until the 1970s. Two buildings deserve particular attention: the swimming pool in Queensway with its parabolic roof, and St John's church at Hilltop, tent-like with dramatic use of coloured glass. In 1986 the A1 road through Hatfield was enlarged to three lanes in each direction and buried in a 'cut-and-cover' tunnel.

Hatfield House, page 75; **Mill Green Museum and Mill**, page 90.

In the locality: Cole Green Way, page 51; Northaw Great Wood, page 53; Symondshyde Picnic Area, page 54.

Hemel Hempstead

Early closing, Wednesday; market days, Thursday, Friday and Saturday.

This is another of Hertfordshire's new towns, like Hatfield and Stevenage, begun in the late 1940s and linked with an existing old town. The picturesque High Street of old Hemel Hempstead had grown along a ridge overlooking the Norman parish church, leading northward towards Piccotts End and Ashridge. On the west side the river Gade skirts old and new town centres and reaches the Bulbourne south of the town. The vast areas of housing which are characteristic of many new towns are here ameliorated by the inclusion of some mature areas at Boxmoor and Leverstock Green.

Church of St Mary, page 63; **Piccotts End Medieval Wall Paintings**, page 77.

In the locality: Cherry Trees Farm, page 51; Grand Union Canal, page 52; The Aubreys, page 55; churches at Flamstead, page 62; Kings Langley, page 64; and Little Gaddesden, page 65; Gorhambury, page 75.

Hertford

Early closing, Thursday; market day, Saturday.

Gascoyne Way, the dual carriageway which cuts rudely through the centre of Hertford, roughly defines the southern limit of the old town. Beyond it, only West Street, reached

The Curfew Tower, St Albans.

(Opposite, above) The church of Holy Cross at Sarratt.

(Opposite, below) The Norman church of St Leonard at Bengeo.

by a subway from St Andrew Street, merits a visit because of its many fine houses of the seventeenth to nineteenth centuries.

Mill Bridge, near the castle gate and civic hall, is a good place to begin a walk around the town. Here the B158 crosses the river Lea. A short distance downstream was the ford which gave Hertford its name. In AD 912 the Saxons' defences against the Danes took the form of two forts, one on each side of the river. They developed into twin towns, with their centres at Old Cross 50 yards (45 metres) to the north-west, and probably near the present town centre to the east. St Andrew Street, beyond Old Cross, is worth exploring for its many fine houses; St Andrew's church, however, was rebuilt in 1869. Hertford Castle lies between St Andrew Street and Castle Street to the south, behind the 1976 civic hall.

The road southward from Mill Bridge leads to Parliament Square, with Hertford's war memorial on its traffic island. The name, which is not ancient, recalls three occasions in the sixteenth century when Parliament met at Hertford Castle to escape the plague. Ahead, beyond Gascoyne Way, are All Saints' church (rebuilt 1893-5), Richard Hale's Grammar School and County Hall. To the left is Fore Street, the town's main business street, which is worth exploring to the end. Notable buildings include an exceptionally rich example of pargeting, James Adams's Shire Hall (about 1770 and restored in the 1980s), and the Salisbury Arms, a Tudor courtyard inn. At the far end of the street are the impressive buildings of Christ's Hospital School, the earliest built in 1695. The school has now moved from these premises. Railway Street, near the east end of Fore Street, leads to the architecturally admired Hertford East railway station and also turns back towards the town centre, passing the Friends' Meeting House.

Salisbury Square has the White Hart (first recorded 1621) and Graveson's distinguished shop front. From here Maidenhead Street leads back towards Mill Bridge. First, however, Bull Plain, on the right, has Dimsdale House (about 1700), the museum and Lombard House (about 1570). Beyond Lombard House a narrow bridge crosses the Lea Navigation ('improved' in 1765) to the

Barge public house and Folly Island, containing a beautifully maintained group of nineteenth-century cottages.

Hertford Nature Walk, page 52; **Friends' Meeting House**, page 63; **Hertford Castle**, page 80; **Hertford Museum**, page 90.

In the locality: Bencroft Wood, page 50; Broxbourne Wood, page 50; Cole Green Way, page 51; Goldings Tree Trail, page 52; Northaw Great Wood, page 53; Paradise Wildlife Park, page 53; Ermine Street, page 56; churches at Bengeo, page 60; Great Amwell, page 62; Little Munden, page 65; and Waterford, page 73; Museum of Street Lighting, page 87. See also Ware, page 46.

Hexton
Ravensburgh Castle, page 57.

Hinxworth
Church of St Nicholas, page 63.

Hitchin
Early closing, Wednesday; market days, Tuesday and Saturday.

Any view of Hitchin should begin with the parish church. The surrounding burial ground is itself enclosed by the 'churchyard', a fringe of shops and houses as in Old St Paul's Churchyard in London. West of the churchyard a small square 'market place' is all that remains of Hitchin's great medieval market area which once was an open space from the churchyard to Bancroft and from Sun Street to Bucklersbury. As in most medieval towns, this was gradually encroached upon as stalls gave way to more permanent premises. The point where the encroachment began can be clearly seen at Moss's Corner in Bancroft. Throughout the nineteenth century this was one of the main markets serving the local cottage industry of straw plaiting: women would purchase their straw here and sell completed plait to dealers. The straw plait industry died about the end of the century; the more conventional market was transferred to St Mary's Square beyond the church in 1939.

The old houses which survive in Hitchin are mostly to be found in the streets mentioned above, and in Bridge Street and Tilehouse Street at their western ends. Opposite the end of Sun Street stands The Priory, built in 1770-7 by Robert Adam for the Radcliffe family, incorporating fragments only of a pre-Reformation Carmelite priory. In the 1980s the building underwent extensive renovation after being disused for several years. South of St Mary's church is The Biggin in Biggin Lane. This building was erected in about 1600 on the site of a Gilbertine priory. It was successively a private residence and a school, and in 1723 it became an almshouse for 'poore auncient or middle aged women', a function which (more kindly described) it continues to perform.

Church of St Mary, page 63; **Hitchin Museum and Art Gallery**, page 91.

In the locality: Icknield Way, page 53; Wilbury Hill, page 54; churches at Great Wymondley, page 62; King's Walden, page 64; Offley, page 66; Pirton, page 67; St Ippollitts, page 70; and St Paul's Walden, page 70; St Paul's Waldenbury, page 77; Chesfield church (ruined), page 79; Minsden Chapel, page 82. See also Stevenage, page 42, and Letchworth, page 33.

The clock-tower at Hoddesdon.

Hoddesdon
Early closing, Thursday; market day, Wednesday.

Ermine Street, the Roman road from London to Ware, became disused north of Enfield in Saxon times and a new route was established a mile (1.6 km) or more to the east along the Lea valley. The relatively large manor of Broxbourne lay on this route by the time of Domesday Book. Hoddesdon developed late along the road north from Broxbourne. It had a market in the thirteenth century and a chapel by 1336. The focal point in the town is the clock house (1835), where a road forks right to Stanstead Abbots. A few attractive houses survive, mainly along the main road south of this junction. North of the clock tower is the Tower shopping centre, more pleasant inside than its exterior leads one to expect, and a massive block of flats of which one hopes that the same may be true. The town centre is now ringed by a one-way road system, seemingly modelled on the racing circuit at nearby Rye House.

Church of St Catherine and St Paul, page 63; **Lowewood Museum**, page 91.

In the locality: Bencroft Wood, page 50; Broxbourne Wood, page 50; Paradise Wildlife Park, page 53; Rye House Marsh Reserve, page 53; Ermine Street, page 56; churches at Great Amwell, page 62; and Stanstead Abbots, page 71; Rye House Gatehouse, page 82; Museum of Street Lighting, page 87. See also Broxbourne, page 18; and Ware, page 46.

Hunsdon
Church of St Dunstan, page 63.

Kelshall
Church of St Faith, page 64.

Kings Langley
The High Street (formerly 'New Chepinge', now the busy A41) has some fine buildings: the Saracen's Head and the gable end of La Caseta restaurant are both sixteenth-century; others are of the seventeenth and eighteenth centuries, many timber-framed with brick façades. Langley Hill, to the west, leads to the site of the thirteenth-century royal pal-

ace, which had on its north side an important Dominican friary. Both sites are now occupied by the Rudolf Steiner School. Nothing of the palace remains above ground; the friary was largely demolished when monastic establishments were dissolved in the sixteenth century, but some fragments, including one substantial building (the locutorium), remain.

Parallel with the High Street on the east side, and accessible via Church Street or The Nap, is the Grand Union Canal and the location of the former mill on the river Gade. The mill house (about 1765) survives. An excellent walk-round guide has been published by the Kings Langley Local History and Museum Society (telephone: 09277 65031). Edmund of Langley, son of Edward III and brother of the Black Prince, died at Kings Langley in 1402. He and his first wife, Isabel of Castile, were buried in a magnificent tomb in the friary church. After the friary was dissolved this tomb was transferred to the parish church.

Church of All Saints, page 64.

In the locality: Cherry Trees Farm, page 51; Grand Union Canal, page 52.

King's Walden
Church of St Mary, page 64.

Knebworth
Church of St Martin, page 64; Knebworth House and Country Park, page 76.

Langley
Minsden Chapel, page 82.

Letchworth
Early closing, Wednesday.
Letchworth is proud to have been the first garden city, where the ideas of Ebenezer Howard were put into practice. Howard sought to create a congenial environment for living by establishing a harmonious relationship between residential, industrial and rural areas. Hampstead Garden Suburb and Welwyn Garden City were later expressions of these ideas. The Letchworth site was selected

and purchased in 1903. It included the greater part of the parishes of Letchworth, Willian and Norton. Barry Parker and Raymond Unwin were appointed architects for the project: their office is preserved as the First Garden City Heritage Museum in an area which contains some of the best of Letchworth's houses. In 1905 a 'Cheap Cottages Exhibition' demonstrated new techniques and styles of building with the erection of 114 dwellings by different architects, none costing more than £150. Most can still be seen in Newells Road, The Quadrant and Icknield Way, the area between the railway and Norton Common. Letchworth is most renowned for the quality of its early housing and the attention which has been given to tree planting in its streets. The quality of design later became more commonplace, and the shopping centre lacks distinction. Some striking industrial buildings survive on the north side of the railway.

The parish churches of Letchworth (St Mary) and Willian (All Saints) lie close together in the extreme south of the town. Norton church (St Nicholas) lies to the northeast. None is of outstanding interest, though St Mary's has an exterior appearance of great charm. More centrally situated in the new town is St George's (1961-4), a novel design by Peter Bosanquet, who also designed Hilltop church in Hatfield.

First Garden City Heritage Museum, page 91; **Letchworth Museum and Art Gallery**, page 94; **Standalone Farm Centre**, page 94.

In the locality: Icknield Way, page 53; Wilbury Hill, page 54; churches at Baldock, page 60; Great Wymondley, page 62; and Weston, page 73; Chesfield church (ruined), page 79. See also Baldock, page 11; Hitchin, page 30; and Stevenage, page 42.

Little Gaddesden
Ashridge Estate, page 49, and House, page 74; church of St Peter and St Paul, page 65.

Little Hadham
Church of St Cecilia, page 65.

(Opposite) The village pump and green at Westmill.

Stocks and a whipping post at Brent Pelham.

Little Hormead
Church of St Mary, page 65.

Little Munden
Church of All Saints, page 65.

London Colney
Two roads enter London Colney from the south. The road from Barnet crosses the river Colne over a seven-arched stone bridge, erected in 1745 by the St Albans and South Mimms Turnpike Trust. Half a mile (800 metres) to the west, just before the road from Shenley crosses the river, there stands All Saints Pastoral Centre within the former Colney Park. The present buildings were begun in 1899 as an Anglican convent. The church added in 1924-7 was designed by Sir Ninian Comper, and finished by his son Sebastian in 1964. The property was purchased in 1973 by the Roman Catholic Church as a pastoral centre. It is not open to casual visitors, but many groups have had an opportunity to participate in activities within its walls. Within the grounds is Chantry Island, the site of a former chantry chapel supposedly on the spot where Alban was arrested prior to his martyrdom, but this has no apparent basis.

In the locality: Shenley Village Cage, page 86; Mosquito Aircraft Museum, page 99.

Markyate
It is difficult to believe that this narrow village street formed part of the A5 main road (Watling Street) until it was bypassed in 1957. It is now a peaceful backwater, evidence of former activity being provided by the numerous inns, interspersed among brick cottages of the eighteenth and nineteenth centuries. The parish church of the same period is situated north of the village on the east side of the main road. It stands in the extensive grounds of a nineteenth-century residence on the site of the medieval nunnery known as Markyate Cell. It was here that the revered Christina of Markyate was the first prioress. After the Dissolution, a mansion was built here by Humphrey Bourchier. A later resident was Katherine, the 'wicked Lady Ferrers', whose exploits as a highwaywoman are particularly associated with Nomansland Common (see page 53).

In the locality: Flamstead church, page 62.

Meesden
Church of St Mary, page 65.

Monken Hadley

Hadley Green and Hadley Common contain many Georgian houses of great distinction, often in delightful combination. Immediately north of Barnet on the A1000 (OS 166: TL 247980) stands an obelisk known familiarly as Hadley Highstone. It was erected in 1749 by Sir Jeremy Sambrooke of Gobions, Brookmans Park, to commemorate the battle of Barnet and the death of the Earl of Warwick near this spot on 14th April 1471. This ensured the victory of Edward IV and the Yorkist faction in the Wars of the Roses.

Church of St Mary, page 65.

In the locality: East Barnet church, page 62; Barnet Museum, page 87.

Much Hadham

Much Hadham is a large village with perhaps the grandest High Street in the county. Development has no doubt been encouraged by the presence next to the church, until early in the nineteenth century, of a palace of the Bishops of London. In 1851 the 250 heads of households in the village included 116 farmers and farmworkers and, surprisingly, 52 tradesmen and shopkeepers and eleven professional people. The remarkable variety of houses of great architectural quality can only be enjoyed on foot, leaving a car at the northern end of the street. The church lies down a lane on the east side.

Church of St Andrew, page 65; **Forge Museum and Victorian Cottage Garden**, page 94.

In the locality: churches at Bishop's Stortford, page 61; Hunsdon, page 63; Little Hadham, page 65; Sawbridgeworth, page 71; and Standon, page 71.

Northchurch

Church of St Mary, page 66.

Nuthampstead

See under Barkway, page 12.

Oxhey

Oxhey Chapel, page 66.

The Pelhams

There are three Pelhams: Furneux, Stocking and Brent. At the time of Domesday Book they were a single estate (Pelham) held by the Bishop of London. In spite of a tradition that Brent (that is, burnt) Pelham suffered a serious fire in the middle ages it could well be that this prefix records instead the method used to clear the forest in that area, whereas Stocking Pelham was cleared by the felling of trees and the removal of their stocks or stumps.

Furneux Pelham is known for its church. 'Time flies, mind your business' is the legend on the clock face; there are cheerful painted angels in the nave roof, Morris and Burne-Jones windows in the south chapel, and the parish chest in the room above the porch could never have been taken up the narrow stairs. The village was also notable for its small brewery (Rayments), which ceased production only in 1987.

Brent Pelham was the home of the legendary Piers Shonks, who slew the Pelham dragon. It is said that this so enraged the Devil that he swore to have Piers 'body and soul, whether buried within the church or out'. This did not appeal to Piers, who arranged in due course that his body should be buried neither inside the church nor outside: his tomb is still there in Brent Pelham church, in an alcove in the thickness of the wall. Outside the church gate at Brent Pelham are the village stocks: only these and the ones at Aldbury are known to survive in Hertfordshire.

In the locality: churches at Anstey, page 59; Buntingford, page 61; Little Hormead, page 65; and Meesden, page 65.

Pirton

Church of St Mary, page 67.

Potters Bar

The name Potters Bar, first recorded in 1387, refers to a former gate between estates along the Great North Road. Farther north were Swanley Bar and Bell Bar. 'Potter' was probably a personal name: Geoffrey le Pottere was living in the parish of South Mimms in 1294. The hamlet of Potters Bar grew with the development of the Great North Road along its eastern side. In 1852 the railway was built ¹/₂ mile (800 metres) to the west and at first Potters Bar station was the only one between

New Barnet and Hatfield. Hadley Wood and Brookmans Park followed in 1885 and 1926 respectively. This ensured the early development of Potters Bar as a favoured residential area for London commuters. The district has few buildings of special architectural interest. West of the station, however, is the so-called Wyllyotts Manor, originally perhaps one of the manor's late medieval barns, now a restaurant.

In the locality: Northaw Great Wood, page 53; Monken Hadley church, page 65.

Puttenham

This is Hertfordshire's most westerly settlement, originating possibly as an estate within the large parish of Tring but later a separate parish, one of the three smallest in the county. Surface irregularities in fields north of the church are evidence for a deserted medieval village: the nearest houses are now remote from the church, and the main centre of population is farther away still at Astrope.

The church (St Mary) is a gem: small, as befits its tiny parish, but grand in conception, with two aisles apparently added in the fourteenth century, and a richly decorated nave roof. The chancel was rebuilt in 1851. A chequer pattern of flint and stone adds distinction to the exterior of the tower. The churchyard and surrounding open countryside provide a fit setting for this charming miniature.

In the locality: Grand Union Canal, page 52.

Radlett

Radlett, astride Watling Street between Elstree and St Albans, has no marked personality but retains considerable dignity. If it had a narrow high street like Markyate it would have been rewarded by now with a bypass; instead the street is wide and the shops have been set back as if shrinking away from the traffic. Radlett has learned to live behind that façade, where there are streets of comfortable houses and an even more remote ring of farms. The railway line from St Pancras to Bedford arrived in 1868. By happy chance the most distinguished buildings which survive in the High Street, a group of flint and brick cottages of 1852, now cluster about the station

approach to welcome returning commuters.

In the locality: Aldenham Country Park, page 49; Aldenham church, page 59; Shenley Village Cage, page 86.

Radwell

Radwell is off the beaten track: the only access to the village passes beneath the A1 north of Baldock. The nineteenth-century church (All Saints) is of no great distinction but should on no account be missed. There are some good brasses and some notable monuments of around 1600, one of which, to the right of the altar, must rate among the county's greatest treasures. This is the poignant memorial in alabaster to Mary Plomer, wife of William Plomer, who died in 1605 'in the 30 year of her age of her XI child'. Mary is portrayed half-length holding her stillborn eleventh child, the others ranged conventionally beneath. The naivety of the carving adds greatly to the strength of emotion which it inspires. William Plomer died twenty years later: he has his own small and more prosaic monument in the nave.

There are fine views around the millpond just below the church, with attractive walks along the Ivel valley.

In the locality: churches at Baldock, page 60; and Hinxworth, page 63.

Redbourn

The iron age settlement later known as The Aubreys may have survived here until the Romans constructed Watling Street a mile (1.6 km) to the east. The Saxons established a settlement between the two, where the church and Old Redbourn still survive. But Watling Street revived as a main road and, as so often happened, the increase in traffic in the later medieval period drew settlers to its verges and established the pattern of the present town. A triangular common which connects Church End with the later developments has many fine houses around its perimeter. Watling Street became the main London-Holyhead road, and Redbourn was an important staging post in the stagecoach era.

Its most characteristic buildings of Georgian red brick include the overpowering Cumberland House (1745) on the common and The Priory and the Red House which face

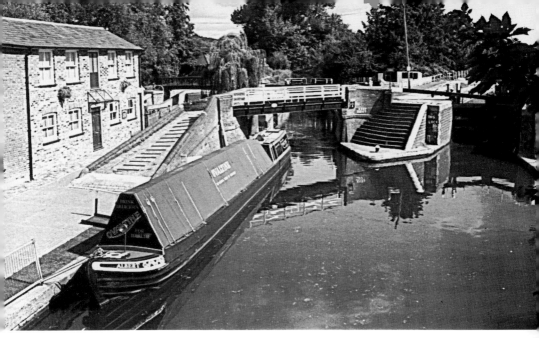

The Batchworth Locks at Rickmansworth.

one another across the High Street. A priory was established here in about 1180, but the present building of that name has no connection with it save that it probably occupies part of the priory land. The establishment of the original priory was bound up with the cult of St Amphibalus, a supposed fugitive Christian priest whom St Alban is said to have assisted, thus bringing about his own martyrdom. Amphibalus is now widely believed not to have existed. Nevertheless, when two burial mounds in Redbourn were opened in 1178 it was in the interests of St Albans Abbey to proclaim that the bones which they contained were those of St Amphibalus. An existing chapel on the site was thereupon enlarged to a small priory to be responsible for the care of these relics, and to be used, apparently, as a rest home for monks from St Albans. It survived until the Dissolution.

The Aubreys, page 55.

In the locality: Ver-Colne Valley Walk, page 54; Flamstead church, page 62; Gorhambury, page 75.

Reed

Unlike all the adjoining villages, each of which has a conventional nucleated centre, Reed has no such focus, though certain concentrations of houses developed in Victorian times. Instead, Reed appears to have been laid out on a grid pattern: buildings are dispersed and roads intersect at right angles. The public house lies on the eastern perimeter, the so-called 'High Street', and the parish church of St Mary is at the southern extremity. (This Saxon building is of great interest: there is beautiful long-and-short work at each of the four corners, and an eleventh-century round-headed north doorway, now blocked.) Reed's grid pattern resembles Roman 'centuriation': the systematic marking out of plots and their allocation for settlement. Although no evidence of Roman occupation has been found in Reed, its location beside Roman Ermine Street lends some plausibility to the view that it could have been such a settlement.

Rickmansworth
Early closing, Wednesday.

For its residents Rickmansworth has the advantage of convenient access to London (by train) and to the countryside. The congested town centre itself does not encourage anyone to linger and has little to offer the visitor. The area of greatest interest lies between the High Street and the river and canal to the south.

The Royston stone is a glacial erratic now sited in the centre of the pedestrian area.

Church Street leads from the High Street to St Mary's church, in which, in spite of its medieval origins, the oldest remaining portion is the tower of 1630. By 1824 the poor state of the rest of the structure necessitated complete rebuilding. It produced, however, an ugly, utilitarian building which was judged by the vestry in 1888 to be 'very unsuitable for Divine Worship'. A further rebuilding was therefore undertaken, preserving only the aisle walls of 1826. Most of the building now visible is the uninspired work of Blomfield in 1890. This is now shared with the Methodist church.

A few other buildings of interest are situated close to the church, notably The Bury, an early seventeenth-century manor house, recently used as offices. It may be viewed from the grounds, which are open to the public. Beyond the church, Church Street leads to the bridge over the river Colne and the Grand Union Canal, with a fine view of Batchworth Locks, where the Rickmansworth Waterways Trust is developing an information and recreational centre, with a programme of events

on summer Sundays. On the other side of the bridge is Rickmansworth's finest building, the mansion of Moor Park.

Rickmansworth Aquadrome, page 53; **Moor Park Mansion,** page 76.

In the locality: Grand Union Canal, page 52; Sarratt church, page 71.

Royston

Early closing, Thursday; market days, Wednesday and Saturday.

At the point where the Roman Ermine Street crossed the Icknield Way an Augustinian priory was established in the twelfth century. In 1189 it obtained the right to hold a weekly market, which is still operating. The priory survived until all monastic establishments were dissolved in 1537, when the priory church was purchased by the townspeople as their parish church. The town of Royston grew up around the market, which would originally have been held at the main crossroads, where there is still a 'middle row' characteristic of former medieval market areas. Royston is supposed to have taken its name from one Lady Roysia of Newsells in Barkway parish, who erected a cross at the road junction, the supposed base of which is still displayed there. ('Roysia's Cross' was the name commonly used for the town until about 1286.)

The narrow High Street is no longer a through road for traffic, but this is part of the line of Ermine Street and in stagecoach days was the route from London to Edinburgh. A large number of inns clustered mainly at the south end, the entrance to the town from London, and also around the crossroads. From 1850 the railway station (London to Cambridge line) at the north end of the town up Kneesworth Street provided a second focus for building development. On the east side of Kneesworth Street are the remains of a 'palace' built here by James I as a hunting lodge in about 1610: all that survives is in fact the rear half of a former double-gabled house. The former Congregational Church Sunday school opposite the palace now houses Royston's museum.

Beneath the south-east side of the crossroads, but with an entrance on the north side of Melbourn Street, is Royston Cave. The priory had been situated in the south-east quadrant of the crossing. Much of the eighteenth- and nineteenth-century development of the town took place in that area, around Fish Hill and Market Hill. There have been many more recent changes, but note the old court house (1849) at the bottom of the hill, and the former corn exchange (1829) at the top. The market moved to this area at about the time when the corn exchange was built. Therfield Heath, to the west of the town, is a nature reserve and contains a barrow cemetery probably of the late neolithic/early bronze age.

Church of St John the Baptist, page 67; **Royston Cave**, page 82; **Royston Museum**, page 95.

In the locality: Therfield Heath, pages 54 and 57; churches at Kelshall, page 64; and Sandon, page 70.

St Albans

Early closing, Thursday; market days, Wednesday and Saturday.

The medieval town

The origin of medieval St Albans lay in the small triangle of streets and alleys outside the abbey's Waxhouse Gate: High Street, Chequer Street, Market Place and French Row. Even by 1800 the built-up area extended to only a few more streets: St Peter's Street to the north, Holywell Hill and Sopwell Lane to the south, George Street (formerly Cook's Row or Church Street) and Fishpool Street towards St Michael's in the west, and Dagnall Street and Spicer Street in the angle between George Street and French Row.

The clock tower, the main focal point of the medieval town, was built 1403-12 to sound a nightly curfew: it is open to the public at limited times (telephone: 0727 60073) and a magnificent view of the cathedral can be had from the top. French Row, Market Street and George Street contain some of the best surviving medieval buildings. The name 'French Row' probably remembers French soldiers who were imprisoned here in 1216, or King John of France, who was lodged at the Fleur-de-Lys after the battle of Poitiers in 1356. St Albans was one of the towns most affected by the Peasants' Revolt in 1381. The building at the corner of French Row and Upper Dagnall Street is identified by a plaque as the former moot hall of the city in which John Ball (one of the main leaders of the revolt) with William Grindecob and other local leaders were tried and condemned.

The Battle of St Albans, 1455

The first battle in the Wars of the Roses was fought in St Albans in May 1455, with Holywell Hill, Chequer Street and St Peter's Street as the front line between the two armies. The Lancastrian army of Henry VI, deployed in St Peter's Street, was attacked by two Yorkist columns advancing up Sopwell Lane and Shropshire Lane (now Victoria Street), both of which had been barricaded. When they were halted by these obstructions a third column under the Earl of Warwick broke through undefended gardens between them in the vicinity of the present London Road. The Lancastrians were routed and one of their leaders, the Duke of Somerset, died on the steps of the Castle Inn at the corner of Shropshire Lane. A second battle of St Albans took place six years later, mostly outside the town to the north, on the road to Sandridge.

A walk round St Albans

Most of the points of interest in St Albans can be seen on this route, and there are many places of refreshment on the way.

It is not always easy to park in the centre of St Albans. The visitor intent on sightseeing and willing to undertake a walk of about 2 miles (3 km) might be wise to use the car park beside St Michael's church and Verulamium Museum. Walk into the adjoining park, across the site of Verulamium. The route between the lake and the river Ver is recommended unless you wish on the same walk to view the remains of the Roman city. At the end of the park cross the river and leave the Fighting Cocks on your left-hand side. This timber-framed building, now a public house, was formerly a dovecote, transferred to its present site in about 1600. The foundations are thought to be part of the perimeter of the former abbey precincts. Take the footpath across the meadow, with a good view of the cathedral on the hill above. You can enter through the chapter house at the south transept. The path to the right leads to Holywell

Hill and an alternative route to the old part of the town, which lies just north of the cathedral.

To return to Verulamium after seeing the old town, walk to the left down George Street and its continuation Fishpool Street, remembering that until 1826 this was the main London-Holyhead road. The well-kept houses, of varying age, and the raised pavements (a protection from the mud on the old road?) make this one of the most attractive streets in the county. At the bottom bear left into St Michael's village, with the Kingsbury watermill on your right. The museum and car park lie ahead.

Beech Bottom Dyke, page 55; **Verulamium**, page 57; **Cathedral and Abbey Church**, page 68; **church of St Michael**, page 70; **church of St Stephen**, page 70; **Gorhambury**, page 75; **Sopwell Nunnery**, page 86; **Kingsbury Watermill Museum**, page 95; **Museum of St Albans**, page 95; **St Albans Organ Museum**, page 97; **Verulamium Museum**, page 97.

In the locality: Nomansland Common, page 53; Symondshyde Picnic Area, page 54; Ver-Colne Valley Walk, page 54; The Aubreys, page 55; Devil's Dyke, page 56; churches at Sandridge, page 71; and Wheathampstead, page 73; the Gardens of the Rose, page 74; Shenley Village Cage, page 86; Mosquito Aircraft Museum, page 99.

St Ippollitts
Church of St Ippolyts, page 70.

St Paul's Walden
Church of All Saints, page 70; St Paul's Waldenbury, page 77.

Sandon
The parish of Sandon consists of several scattered settlements here known as 'ends' or 'greens'. Church End has all the features of a typical village centre: the parish church, a former public house (closed 1987), a green with adjoining pond (but this one has geese, not ducks), and the bury or manor house with seventeenth-century façade and dovecote and a well-documented thirteenth-century barn. Half a mile (800 metres) to the west is Roe Green, a large open space ringed by houses

which are served by individual spurs from the road which crosses the centre. This is the green which provides for parish sport and recreation. Other 'ends' lie south of the church on the road to Buntingford.

Church of All Saints, page 70.

In the locality: Icknield Way, page 53; churches at Kelshall, page 64; and Wallington, page 72.

Sandridge
Church of St Leonard, page 71.

Sarratt
The long village green is a more intimate version of Roe Green in the parish of Sandon. The buildings around the perimeter approach more closely and invite inspection. There are flint cottages, timber-framed houses and some brick façades, with two public houses, a pump, at least one surviving pond and several pond depressions. Holy Cross church stands apart, with the 1821 almshouses nearby. This will remain one of west Hertfordshire's most attractive villages as long as a proper balance can be retained between old and new.

Church of the Holy Cross, page 71.

In the locality: Cherry Trees Farm, page 51; Whippendell Woods, page 54.

Sawbridgeworth
Early closing, Thursday.

Sawbridgeworth contains some excellent individual buildings, but its outstanding quality lies in the street scenes as a whole: the compositions and glimpses of secret corners which are presented to the viewer who strolls around these streets. A major contribution to this effect is the scale of Sawbridgeworth: streets are comfortably narrow, few houses have more than two storeys, traffic within the town is moderate. The London Road (A1184) mercifully carries through traffic past on the west side of the centre. Turn off into Bell Street, leave the car in the (usually) adequate car park and take to the pavement. Notice The Elms next door, The Red House opposite. Walk slowly down to Knight Street (Market House on the corner) and enjoy the view to the left. The church lies ahead. Market Square and Fair Green beckon to the right. An excellent walk-round guide is published

Church End, Sandon. (The Six Bells is now a private house.)

by the Local History Society (telephone: 0279 722557).

Church of Great St Mary, page 71.

In the locality: churches at Bishop's Stortford, page 61; and Much Hadham, page 65; Bishop's Stortford Local History Museum, page 87; Rhodes Memorial Museum, page 87; Forge Museum and Victorian Cottage Garden, page 94.

Shenley

Shenley lies south of St Albans, midway between the A5 (Watling Street) and the A6 (the London-Holyhead road). Its village street, Shenley Lane, joins the road from London before making a modest entry into St Albans. The village therefore has been spared heavy through traffic. Grouped at its centre are two public houses, the village pond, the former cage or lock-up and the site of the pound for stray animals. The former parish church, St Botolph's, at the north end of the village was declared redundant in 1972 and is now a private residence.

A very strong local tradition identified Salisbury Hall, 1 mile (1.6 km), outside the village, close to the London road, as the place where King Charles II established his mistress Nell Gwynne, and the location, remote but close to London, would certainly have been convenient for such a purpose. The

house was acquired and largely rebuilt in 1669 by Jeremy Snow, a banker possibly acting as an agent for the king: he received a baronetcy in 1679. The house is not open to the public, but its grounds now accommodate the Mosquito Aircraft Museum. A later resident of Shenley was the architect Nicholas Hawksmoor, pupil and colleague of Sir Christopher Wren. His house, Porters Park, survives much altered among the outbuildings of Shenley Hospital. His tomb is in the private section of the former churchyard.

Shenley Village Cage, page 86; **Mosquito Aircraft Museum**, page 99.

Standon

A vast parish, Standon contains, in addition to the village of Standon, the hamlets of Puckeridge, Colliers End and High Cross, all of which have grown up along the old North Road (now the A10). Puckeridge, now bypassed, stands where formerly the main road forked left for Royston and the north, right for Barkway and Cambridge. Standon village has little through traffic, but an immensely wide street which formerly accommodated a weekly market and a twice yearly fair.

The eminence of Standon has derived from two sources: the power of the families (Clares in the middle ages and Sadleirs since 1539) who held the principal manor (the Lordship);

and until the Reformation the Order of St John of Jerusalem, to whom the church at Standon and 140 acres (57 hectares) of land were granted by Gilbert de Clare late in the twelfth century. The order established here a commandery (now lost), a hospice and a school, and it has been suggested that this might have been the large building, timber-framed with brick nogging, which stands immediately south of the churchyard and was until the 1960s the village school. It is now known as Knights' Court. This is little more than speculation, and the discovery of massive medieval timbers in two houses in the main street, one of them the post office, suggests a possible alternative location. Standon Lordship, partly surviving from 1546 but largely rebuilt, lies close to the river Rib about a mile (1.6 km) to the south. It can be glimpsed from the road to Barwick.

Standon extends west of the A10, where at Old Hall Green is the Roman Catholic St Edmund's College. This had originated as a Roman Catholic school in Hampshire, where its position became untenable as a result of anti-Catholic feeling following the Jacobite rising of 1745. In 1753 it was re-established at Standon, first at the Lordship, which was at the time empty and available for letting. When it was sold in 1767 the school had to find new accommodation and, after a short sojourn at Hare Street, acquired in 1769 the property at Old Hall Green which became the nucleus of the present much enlarged establishment. In 1793 the academy, as it was by then called, received an influx of refugees from the English College of Douai in Flanders, whence they had been evicted by revolutionary guards. The college has become a major centre for Roman Catholic education in England.

A turning on the west side of the A10 south of St Edmund's College leads to Standon Green End. Here, in a field behind Great Mead on the south side of the road (OS 166: TL 364197), is the 'Balloon Stone', a sandstone boulder which marks the spot where the pioneer balloonist Vincenzo Lunardi completed the first balloon flight in England on 15th September 1784. He had ascended from the Artillery Ground at Finsbury, north London, and reached this point after 2 hours and

15 minutes, having first touched ground briefly in a field at North Mymms. Local farm labourers were naturally scared by this apparition, but an early arrival was William Baker of Bayfordbury, who entertained Lunardi at his home. He also caused this stone to be moved to the spot from Bengeo Street, where it had lain beside the roadway, and had a brass plate mounted on it to commemorate the descent (photograph, page 8). The present plate is a facsimile of the original, substituted in 1875 by Arthur Giles Puller of Youngsbury (who also erected the Clarkson memorial at Wadesmill). A public footpath enters the field opposite Knoll Farm.

Church of St Mary, page 71.

In the locality: churches at Braughing, page 61; Buntingford, page 61; Little Hadham, page 65; Little Munden, page 65; and Much Hadham, page 65; Forge Museum and Victorian Garden, page 94.

Stanstead Abbots

Rye House Marsh Reserve, page 53; church of St James, page 71; Rye House Gatehouse, page 82.

Stevenage

Early closing, Wednesday; market days, Thursday, Friday and Saturday.

The earliest settlement at Stevenage developed around the site of the parish church. By the thirteenth century the road half a mile (800 metres) to the west, later the Great North Road, was already developing as a main road from London to the North, and the traffic and trade which this brought caused a movement of population towards the road. It became the High Street of what is now 'Old Stevenage'. From the Bowling Green at the north end of this street a footpath known as The Avenue provides an attractive walk to the church. The north end of the High Street still accommodates an annual street fair in September. Old Stevenage High Street has the usual 'middle row': an island of small shops where once there would have been market stalls. A small weekly street market continued to be held in this area until it was transferred to the New Town in 1959.

The focal centre of Stevenage has now moved again, from Old Town to New Town.

The Avenue, Stevenage.

Stevenage was the first town to be designated such in 1946; the first houses were occupied in 1951 and the new town centre was completed in 1957. A feature of the design is the network of cycleways, independent of roads, around the town centre. The new town has incorporated the former separate parish of Shephall, which retains some of its village character. Also within the new town area, beside the roundabout south of the railway station, are the 'Six Hills', a line of supposed Romano-British burial mounds which were for a long time a landmark beside the Great North Road as it approached Stevenage ('Old Stevenage') from London.

Church of St Nicholas, page 71; **Stevenage Museum**, page 99.

In the locality: churches at Benington, page 60; Cottered, page 61; Great Wymondley, page 62; Knebworth, page 64; St Ippollitts, page 70; Walkern, page 72; and Weston, page 73; Benington Lordship Gardens, page 74; Knebworth House and Country Park, page 76; Chesfield church (ruined), page 79; Cromer Windmill, page 79. See also Hitchin, page 30, and Letchworth, page 33.

Tewin

This must have been an early settlement by the Saxon invaders: the name commemorates the pagan god Tiw. The parish church, splendidly isolated half a mile (800 metres) southwest of the village, dates from about 1100, but with a great deal of later alteration. In the churchyard is the famous tomb of Ann Grimston (1713), riven by the roots and trunk of a tree growing from within. She is supposed to have said that life after death was as likely as that a tree would sprout from her grave: but that story was no doubt concocted to explain the tree!

The sale of the Cowper estates here in 1919 exposed the village to building development and a great increase in population. In the extreme north the parish extends across the road from Bramfield to Bull's Green. At the point where this road passes through Canon's Wood (OS 166: TL 280166) there stands at the roadside a squared timber post over 6 feet (2 metres) high. It is inscribed 'Clibbon's Post. Dec. 28 1782'. At this spot, and on that day, Walter Clibbon, a notorious footpad of Wareside, was shot dead when he and two of

Clibbon's Post, Tewin.

his sons attacked Mr Ben Whittenbury of nearby Queen Hoo, who with his son and a servant was searching for them after they had robbed other members of the Whittenbury family. Clibbon's body was taken to the Horns public house at Bull's Green, where it lay overnight in the barn which still stands next to the house.

In the locality: Digswell church, page 61; Digswell Viaduct, page 80.

Therfield

Therfield is one of Hertfordshire's most attractive villages. To see its best features start at the triangular village green, where shop and public house stand side by side. A cul-de-sac opposite leads past The Limes to the parish church (St Mary's). The church itself holds no great interest. Nave and chancel were virtually rebuilt in 1873-8, owing to the dangerous condition of the old building, and the tower was added in 1911. The few survivals from the former church include a fine cedarwood monument to Ann Turner

(died 1677).

The group of thatched houses at Churchgate is visually the most exciting in the village. The old rectory, in private occupation, lies down a short lane to the south: it contains work of the fifteenth century, including a former chapel. Immediately to the right inside the churchyard a footpath leads past Therfield's first schoolhouse into Pedlar's Lane. From here the lane to the right returns to the green, passing the impressively timber-framed Old Forge House. The forge which once stood in front of it is now demolished. A longer walk to the left up Pedlar's Lane leads to the ridge road, with magnificent views over Cambridgeshire. Turn left here past the former Bell, a private residence since 1991; after a few yards a footpath to the left leads back to the west end of the churchyard, passing first Tuthill Manor, a timber-framed building spectacularly restored from complete decay, and beyond it a field in which can be seen the turf-covered remains of Therfield's short-lived twelfth-century castle.

Therfield Heath, pages 54 and 57.
In the locality: Kelshall church, page 64.

Throcking

Church of Holy Trinity, page 72.

Thundridge

Like Tewin, Thundridge derives its name from a pagan god ('Thunor's ridge'), indicating an early settlement. This settlement would have commanded the point where Ermine Street crossed the river Rib at what is now known as Wadesmill (a name which is first recorded in the thirteenth century). Old Thundridge lay half a mile (800 metres) to the east on the south side of the river, where the ruined tower (OS 166: TL 368173) is all that survives of the old parish church, abandoned in 1853. It occupies a formerly moated site and can be reached by walking along Old Church Lane from the bottom of the village street near Wadesmill bridge. The main road formerly came through this village and crossed the river eastward of the present bridge, which was built in 1824-6.

Drivers going north on the A10 road from Wadesmill will notice on the west side of the hill a low stone obelisk. It bears the following inscription:

> On the spot where stands this monument, in the month of June 1785, Thomas Clarkson resolved to devote his life to bringing about the abolition of the slave trade. Placed here by Arthur Giles Puller of Youngsbury, 1879.

Clarkson was a Quaker, born at Wisbech in 1760. He subsequently became the driving force behind the movement of which William Wilberforce was the political figurehead.

In the locality: churches at Little Munden, page 65; and Standon, page 71.

Tring

Early closing, Wednesday; market day, Friday (cattle, Monday).

Tring is a bustling little town, now bypassed, situated in the Bulbourne Gap through the Chilterns, on Roman Akeman Street. From 1873 to 1938 Tring Park and its estate, which included a large part of the town, was the property of the Rothschild family, who were generous benefactors. Their two most obvious creations were the Rose and Crown inn (1905), 'an early and lavish example of the

The zebra-head pavement at Tring recalls Walter Rothschild's interest in zoology.

pseudo-half-timbered inn', which Nikolaus Pevsner found so deplorable, and the Walter Rothschild Zoological Museum. Nowadays Tring is largely a commuter dormitory. With most through traffic diverted, its apparent busyness is due more to the narrowness of its twisting, hilly High Street than to the volume of traffic passing through. The parish church has some grandeur but little charm. Many old houses, mostly of the Victorian period, remain, and alleys and courtyards off the High Street invite exploration.

Church of St Peter and St Paul, page 72; **Walter Rothschild Zoological Museum**, page 99.

In the locality: Ashridge Estate, page 49; Grand Union Canal, page 52; Tring Reservoirs National Nature Reserve, page 54; Northchurch church, page 66; Ashridge House, page 74.

Walkern

Church of St Mary, page 72.

Wallington

Church of St Mary, page 72.

Waltham Cross

Waltham Cross takes its name from the memorial which King Edward I caused to be erected here in 1290. His wife, Queen Eleanor, had died in Lincolnshire, and her funeral cortege took thirteen days to reach Westminster Abbey. A cross was erected at each overnight resting place: they survive only at Geddington, Northampton and Waltham, with a Victorian replica at Charing (now in the forecourt of Charing Cross station). The cross at Waltham stands not at the abbey on the Essex side of the river Lea, where the queen's body must undoubtedly have lain, but at the point where the road to the abbey left the London road. The cross has been much restored and is now overshadowed by the massive multi-storey car park and shopping centre. The Four Swans Inn, which formerly occupied part of this site, has been demolished, but its gallows-type inn sign still spans the road north of the cross, in an area which has been pedestrianised. The three-dimensional swans which it carries are modern copies of eighteenth-century predecessors, two of which are preserved in the Lowewood Museum (page 91).

In the locality: Capel Manor Educational Farm, page 50; Cedars Park, page 51; Capel Manor Gardens, page 74; Temple Bar, page 86. See also Cheshunt, page 19

Ware

Early closing, Thursday; market day, Tuesday.

This is where the Roman Ermine Street crossed the river Lea. It was the scene of a famous encounter between King Alfred and the Danes in AD 895, and a trading rival to Hertford in the middle ages. A major source of wealth in the eighteenth and nineteenth centuries was the malting industry, whose characteristic buildings, mostly converted to other purposes, continue to enliven the townscape. In the 1970s a viaduct was built to carry the A10 across the valley, removing most through traffic from the town. In spite of the sad loss of many of its old buildings, Ware retains a great deal to interest the visitor.

The car park next to the public library at the west end of the High Street provides a convenient starting point for a perambulation. Opposite is St Mary's parish church, mostly of the fourteenth century but much restored. Behind the High Street on its north side runs West Street: number 2 has the remains of a thirteenth-century timber frame, partly visible from the pavement, exceptionally old for a domestic building. The south side of the High Street is notable for its long narrow burgage plots running back to the river. Many wagon entries have been incorporated in the houses on this side of the street, and in the sides of some of them can be seen the characteristic 'service' doorways of the former hall-houses of which these timbers formed a part, perhaps in different locations.

In East Street, which matches West Street behind the east end of the High Street, a similar entry gives access to Blue Coat Yard. On the right in this yard is Place House, possibly one of Ware's two Domesday manor houses, rebuilt in the thirteenth century as a magnificent aisled hall, most of which remains. In the 1680s this building was purchased by the governors of Christ's Hospital as a school for the boys who were being

fostered in Ware. The cottages on the opposite side of the yard were built in 1698 as living accommodation: each housed a foster mother and up to fourteen boys. The Ware Blue Coat boys continued at Place House until 1761, when they were transferred to Hertford.

Follow the curve of the High Street to cross the river at Bridgefoot. On the upstream side of the bridge are some attractive eighteenth-century gazebos belonging to the houses in the High Street. Many, lately sadly dilapidated, are gradually being restored. On the south side of the river is the site of the great Victoria Malting (destroyed by fire in the 1980s) and a boatyard. A footpath runs along the river bank to a footbridge which returns to the car park. A small gate here gives access to the pleasant public garden behind the so-called Priory, once a Franciscan friary of which few traces remain. The present building houses council offices.

Scott's Grotto, page 82; **Ware Museum**, page 100.

In the locality: Rye House Marsh Reserve, page 53; churches at Great Amwell, page 62; Hunsdon, page 63; Little Munden, page 65; Much Hadham, page 65; Standon, page 71; and Stanstead Abbots, page 71; Rye House Gatehouse, page 82; Museum of Street Lighting, page 87; Forge Museum and Victorian Cottage Garden, page 94 See also Hertford, page 27; and Hoddesdon, page 31.

Waterford

Goldings Tree Trail, page 52; church of St Michael and All Angels, page 73.

Watford

Early closing, Wednesday; market days, Tuesday, Friday and Saturday.

During the nineteenth century the arrival of the railway and new industries transformed Watford from a country market town to the largest industrial centre in Hertfordshire. Ancient road patterns have now been disrupted by new roads and traffic systems which make this a particularly confusing place for visitors. Until the mid nineteenth century Watford was a one-street town. The main road from London passed under the railway bridge (1837) and crossed the river Colne at the southern end. It continued in a north-westerly direction as the High Street, past the parish church, until at the end of the town the St Albans road struck off across the fields to the right to Watford station (later Watford Junction). The High Street continued towards Berkhamsted as the Hempstead Road. Most of Watford's surviving buildings of merit are in the immediate vicinity of the church, notably the five-gabled Bedford almshouses (1580) to the west, and the Fuller/Chilcott school (1704) to the south. The buildings of the former Benskins Brewery have become the town museum.

Cassiobury Park, page 51; **Cheslyn Gardens**, page 74; **Watford Museum**, page 100.

In the locality: Aldenham Country Park, page 49; Cherry Trees Farm, page 51; Grand Union Canal, page 52; Ver-Colne Valley Walk, page 54; Whippendell Woods, page 54; churches at Aldenham, page 59; Kings Langley, page 64; and Sarratt, page 71; Ox-hey Chapel, page 66; Moor Park Mansion, page 76.

Welwyn
Early closing, Wednesday and Saturday.
At the heart of Welwyn is a rectangle of four streets: High Street, Church Street, Mill Lane and Prospect Place. The parish church (St Mary's) stands at the corner of High Street and Church Street. It has suffered successive catastrophes: drastic restorations in 1824, 1868-70 and 1910-11, which replaced most of what had gone before, were followed in 1952 by a serious case of arson which necessitated the rebuilding of the east wall and re-furnishing of the chancel. There survives a fragment of thirteenth-century moulding in the north wall of the chancel, a fifteenth-century double piscina and, miraculously, the fifteenth-century rood screen which now stands against the north wall of the chancel. The church looks across to the Wellington public house, formerly a busy coaching inn, which under its earlier name (the Swan) is referred to as early as 1352. At one time the Great North Road passed through the High Street and Church Street. Nowadays the A1 motorway runs half a mile (800 metres) to the east, and Welwyn is relatively undisturbed.

Next door to the Wellington on its north side is Ivy Cottage (about 1450) which in the 1870s was Miss Applegarth's school. Ann Van Gogh taught French there and lodged at Rose Cottage in Church Street. Her brother Vincent is said to have visited her there. Beyond Ivy Cottage is Guessens, where Dr Edward Young, rector of Welwyn and highly regarded poet ('Night Thoughts'), lived from 1730 to 1765. Church Street has some fine houses and an early Victorian shop front opposite the church, once Welwyn's principal grocer's shop. Next to the churchyard on the north side of the street is Church House (late fifteenth century). The village fire engine house once stood in this corner of the church-yard, and beneath the eaves of the house there still rests the fire hook with which burning thatch would have been removed.

At the end of the street a red brick house stands beside a solitary gatepost: it is difficult now to visualise that this was once the lodge at the entrance to the drive of Lockleys, now on the far side of the motorway. Before 1717 this was the road to Hertford. Mill Lane, which turns south out of Church Street, provides a pleasant walk through to Prospect Place. The present cul-de-sac to the left at the end took over as the main Hertford road from 1717 to 1906. Prospect Place leads back past the civic centre and the present Hertford Road to the High Street. The White Hart stands on the corner, well placed to greet coaches when they entered the village from London.

Welwyn Roman Baths, page 58.

In the locality: Ayot Greenway, page 50; churches at Ayot St Lawrence, page 59; Ayot St Peter, page 60; Digswell, page 61; and Knebworth, page 64; Knebworth House and Country Park, page 76; Shaw's Corner, page 78; Digswell Viaduct, page 80.

Welwyn Garden City
Early closing, Wednesday.
This was the second of Hertfordshire's two Garden Cities (see also Letchworth, page 33). The first land was acquired in 1919, and building began in Handside Lane in the following year. A temporary railway 'halt' was provided in 1920 and the present station in 1926. Welwyn Stores opened in temporary premises in 1921 and moved to the present building (now John Lewis's) in 1939. Howard's idea

of a garden city required easy access to nature and a separation of residential from industrial areas. At Welwyn Garden City the main railway line provides a convenient demarcation line: industries lie mainly on the east side, facing the central shopping and commercial area on the west. Around them are residential areas, with a main north-south axis parallel to the railway which incorporates extensive planted areas. Major public open spaces have been preserved or developed in the north-west (Sherrardspark Wood) and south (Stanborough Lakes Recreation Area).

To see the best of Welwyn Garden City drive through from north to south, starting at the Welwyn-Hertford Road (B1000). Between A1 and Digswell Viaduct (see page 80) turn south at the roundabout into Bessemer Road and subsequently into Digswell Road, signposted to the town centre. This section is best seen in May when the cherry trees are in blossom. After crossing the ornamental bridge over a now disused railway line the road descends to the Campus, giving a fine view ahead down Parkway. After skirting the Campus continue to the far end of Parkway and along Stanborough Road to the sailing lake (or return via Lemsford Lane and Handside Lane).

In the locality: Ayot Greenway, page 50; Cole Green Way, page 51; Symondshyde Picnic Area, page 54; Welwyn Roman Baths, page 58; churches at Ayot St Lawrence, page 59; Ayot St Peter, page 60; Digswell, page 61; Knebworth, page 64; and Wheathampstead, page 73; Knebworth House and Country Park, page 76; Shaw's Corner, page 78; Digswell Viaduct, page 80; Mill Green Museum and Mill, page 90.

Westmill

Many people would include this among Hertfordshire's most attractive villages. There is not very much here, but what there is is perfect: the very fine houses in the main street, the terrace of cottages beyond the church (Saxon in origin) and the trim green at the south-west end make a modest but harmonious group. 2 miles (3 km) away at Cherry Green is Button Snap, once the property of Charles Lamb (see page 103). The lane beyond Button Snap leads to the deserted medieval village of Wakeley. At the time of Domesday Book its population might have been as many as 45; now there is one farmhouse.

In the locality: churches at Braughing, page 61; and Buntingford, page 61.

Weston
Church of Holy Trinity, page 73.

Wheathampstead
This is where the Roman road from Verulamium to Baldock crossed the river Lea. It later became an important road junction on the road between St Albans and Hitchin. The iron age hillfort now known as Devil's Dyke lay ½ mile (800 metres) to the east. The village is graced by a beautiful parish church, the impressive Bull inn, now a restaurant, and at Bury Green the former National School, built in 1862 to replace an earlier building, and now converted to offices. This is a most attractive example of the use of polychrome brickwork.

Devil's Dyke, page 56; **church of St Helen**, page 73.

In the locality: Ayot Greenway, page 50; Lea Valley Walk, page 53; Nomansland Common, page 53; Symondshyde Picnic Area, page 54; churches at Ayot St Lawrence, page 59; Ayot St Peter, page 60; and Sandridge, page 71; Shaw's Corner, page 78.

Wyddial
Church of St Giles, page 73.

3
The Hertfordshire countryside

There are ample opportunities for access to the Hertfordshire countryside: many volumes of suggested walks have been published. The Countryside Management Service (CMS), sponsored by Hertfordshire County Council, local district and borough councils and the Countryside Commission, has developed recreational paths and sites throughout the county, several of which are described here. The Service also organises 'Stepping Out', a year-round programme of events exploring the local countryside. Details about these and the other aspects of the CMS may be obtained from the Countryside Information Officer, Planning and Environment Department, County Hall, Hertford SG13 8DN (telephone: 0992 555257).

The county also has a large number of nature reserves and nature trails, many of them administered by the Hertfordshire and Middlesex Wildlife Trust (HMWT). A selection of these is also included below. Further information may be obtained from the Trust at Grebe House, St Michael's Street, St Albans AL3 4SN (telephone: 0727 58901). Grebe House, an old timber-framed building rescued from demolition in Watford and re-erected here, is situated beside the Verulamium car park (see page 57). It contains a shop and wildlife interpretative centre, with displays relating to wildlife in the area.

The following descriptions of walks and sites indicate whether further information may be obtained from CMS or HMWT.

Aldenham Country Park, Dagger Lane, Elstree AL2 2NR (OS 166: TQ 166961). Telephone: 081-953 9602. CMS. The entrance is in Aldenham Road, a turning off A411 west of Elstree.

The country park was established in 1971 on land which was formerly part of Aldenham Common, but farmed in the nineteenth century. The main feature of the park is the reservoir, hand-dug by French prisoners of war in the 1790s to provide a means of maintaining the levels of surrounding rivers following the construction of the Grand Junction Canal. It is now used solely for recreational purposes, and by waterfowl. A lakeside nature trail has been developed, and the park contains several rare breeds of domestic animals including a herd of longhorn cattle. Woodland contains a variety of tree species. Facilities include a picnic area with lavatories and a children's adventure playground. In 1992 the country park was awarded visitor centre status by the Rare Breeds Survival Trust.

Ashridge Estate, Little Gaddesden. National Trust. Telephone: 0442 85227.
Monument, shop and information centre open daily, April to October, afternoons only. Woodlands open at all times.

When Lord Brownlow's Ashridge property (see page 74) was broken up in 1921, a large part was acquired by the National Trust, later extended to over 4000 acres (1600 hectares). The area is generally open to the public, subject to the observance of bylaws. The Bridgewater Monument, which was erected in 1832 to commemorate the achievements of the third Duke of Bridgewater, known as the 'Canal Duke' for his work in pioneering the construction of canals, affords wide views over the countryside. It also makes a convenient focal point (OS 165: SP 970131): there is a National Trust shop and information office nearby. This is also the starting point of a nature trail of about 1½ miles (2.4 km), about which an excellent pamphlet guide can be obtained at the shop.

Ashridge House can be seen from the road end of the drive that leads up to the monument.

Ayot Greenway, Ayot St Peter (OS 166: TL 222144). CMS. Car parking at Ayot station.

This is a footpath which uses a section of the disused Luton, Dunstable and Welwyn Junction Railway (1860-1966). The path starts at the former Ayot station and runs westward for about 2 miles (3 km) to Blackbridge, where it terminates on Sheepcote Lane. There are several access points en route. The rich flora is particularly attractive to a variety of butterflies.

Bencroft Wood, Broxbourne (OS 166: TL 331064). CMS. 2 miles (3 km) west of Broxbourne.

This old wood consists in the main of coppiced hornbeam. Coppicing is to be continued in selected areas. There are a few oak trees and former clearings have been colonised by silver birch. Footpaths have been laid out from the two car parking areas provided.

Broxbourne Wood (OS 166: TL 328069). CMS. Two car parks in Pembridge Lane.

82 acres (33 hectares) here form part of the Wormley Woods Site of Special Scientific Interest. There is a picnic area and several walking routes. Vegetation includes Norway spruce, birch and hornbeam. Streamsides give added variety both in flora and in birdlife: cuckoos, warblers, winter flocks of finches and most species of tits can be seen. Muntjac deer also use the wood.

Capel Manor Educational Farm, Theobalds Park, Waltham Cross (OS 166: TL 343007). Telephone: 0992 763849. The farm is located within the grounds of Theobalds Park, 400 yards (350 metres) from Temple Bar.

Open afternoons at weekends and in school holidays from April to October. School parties by arrangement.

There is a wide range of livestock and a continuous breeding programme which makes

Longhorn cattle at Aldenham Country Park.

The Bridgewater Monument on the Ashridge Estate.

it likely that young chicks or piglets will be on show for visitors. Some rare breeds are kept and demonstrations of milking can be seen daily. Capel Manor Gardens (see page 74) are nearby.

Cassiobury Park, Watford. Watford Borough Council. Telephone: 0923 226400, extension 2501.

These 237 acres (96 hectares) of parkland border on their west side the Grand Union Canal and the river Gade. In addition to the usual recreational facilities and a miniature railway there is ample space for walks, which are particularly attractive in the river/canal area. Public footpaths cross the canal at Iron Bridge Lock and continue half a mile (800 metres) across the golf course to Whippendell Woods (page 54). Access to Cassiobury Park can be obtained from many points on the perimeter, particularly from Parkside Drive and Cassiobury Park Avenue.

HMWT has sponsored a nature trail 1¼ miles (2 km) long and taking about one hour, starting from the car park in Gade Avenue (leaflet available).

Cedars Park, Theobalds Lane, Waltham Cross. Broxbourne Borough Council.

The Cedars, now a public park, occupies part of the site of the former manor of Theobalds. Some features of successive buildings are identified, but the main interest lies in the well-maintained gardens. An excellent 'trail' has been devised, with a printed guide obtainable on site which incorporates both historical and botanical information.

Cherry Trees Farm, Ollieberrie Lane, Belsize, Sarratt (OS 166: TL 030012). Telephone: 09232 68289.
Open Wednesdays to Sundays.

This farm of 40 acres (16 hectares) has a variety of livestock, many of rare breeds, including pigs, sheep, cattle and poultry, as well as working horses. There is also a small acreage of wheat or barley and vegetables. The use of organic farming methods results in an exceptionally varied wildlife. Visitors, who are welcome both individually and in pre-booked groups, find themselves closely involved in the activities of the farm.

Cole Green Way, Hertingfordbury (OS 166: TL 285111). CMS.

This footpath follows the line of the disused Hertford and Welwyn Junction Railway, which closed in 1966. The path crosses

The Aylesbury arm of the Grand Union Canal at Dixon's Gap, near Tring.

open country between Hertford in the east and the A414 near Cole Green in the west. The former Cole Green station, now devoid of all buildings, is a pleasant picnic site en route. The total length is about 4 miles (6 km), but there are several intermediate access points. Access in Hertford is from West Street, just below County Hall. The way terminates at the busy A414, whence Deadfield Lane, an old drovers' track 100 yards to the south, leads back to Letty Green. However, it may be more convenient to leave the footpath half a mile (800 metres) before reaching the A414, where it passes the Cowper Arms.

Goldings Tree Trail (OS 166: TL 312142). CMS. On A119 just north of Hertford. Use the southern entrance, nearest to Hertford.

The trail, identifying twenty species, has been developed in the grounds of Goldings Estate. It starts from the car park. An identification guide is available from CMS.

Grand Union Canal

The Grand Union Canal enters Hertfordshire south of Puttenham and follows a route roughly parallel with the A41, on its north side, via Tring Station, Berkhamsted and Watford, after which it veers south-westerly to Rickmansworth. The full length of the towpath can be walked, but the section between Northchurch and Tring has been developed particularly to demonstrate its recreational possibilities, with an attractive canalside walk and appropriate maintenance and conservation projects. There is convenient access from Berkhamsted and Tring stations. (See also Rickmansworth, page 37.)

Hertford Nature Walk. Devised by HMWT and Royal Society for Protection of Birds. (No leaflet available.)

The walk lies within the riverside meadows of the Lea and Beane, between Hertford canal basin (The Folly) and St Leonard's church, Bengeo. The full distance is about 2 miles (3 km). The best starting point is the car park at Hartham swimming pool, near the bottom of Port Hill. Walk towards the swimming pool; then turn left across the footbridge over the river Beane, for a clockwise circuit via St Leonard's church, the river Lea footbridge, Hertford lock and the canal basin. Alternatively, turn to the right at the swimming pool across a 'dummy' footbridge which leads to the canal basin and the anticlockwise circuit. Of chief interest in the Beane are crayfish and, at the footbridge, water celery; on the Lea the birdlife, particularly among the old groves of willows. Boating activity and canal structures along the Lee Navigation provide additional interest. The cottages at The Folly and the canalside Barge public house also have their attractions.

Icknield Way (OS 166: TL 132300).

Britain's oldest long-distance path is still accessible to walkers, though part of it has now been built over. One of the most enjoyable stretches across open country is the Telegraph Hill section, starting from a convenient parking lay-by on the south side of B655 east of Pegsdon and continuing about 4 miles (6 km) south-westerly towards Dray Ditches and the Barton-Luton road (A6). A circular route can be devised without too much difficulty. An 'Icknield Way Regional Trail' has also been designated, diverging from the traditional route and avoiding the A505. It provides separate routes for walkers (via Wallington, Sandon and Therfield) and for riders (via Pirton and Ashwell). A leaflet is available from CMS.

Lea Valley Walk. CMS.

A regional route for walkers, from the source of the river Lea at Luton to its exit into the Thames in east London, is being planned. (A new leaflet is being prepared.) The Harpenden-Batford section runs for 2 miles (3 km) parallel to the A6129 (Luton to Wheathampstead) on its western side, making good use of the disused route of the Hatfield, Luton and Dunstable Railway, closed in 1965. Access at the north end is from Westfield Road, Harpenden. The path then follows the railway, with a diversion down to the river between Pickford bridge and Batford mill, then on to Aldwickbury and Leasybridge. There are many intermediate opportunities to return to Lower Luton Road.

Nomansland Common, Wheathampstead (OS 166: TL 171124). Nomansland Common lies mainly on the west side of the B651 road between Wheathampstead and Sandridge. Car park off Ferrers Lane.

The place is so named because it lies on the border between land held by the abbeys of St Albans and Westminster. The boundary between Wheathampstead and Sandridge parishes passes across it. This is also the area associated in the seventeenth century with the exploits of 'wicked Lady Ferrers', the legendary highwaywoman (hence the Wicked Lady public house). The common, formerly grazed, is now used mainly for recreation. It is owned by Wheathampstead Parish Council and Lord Spencer and is managed by CMS.

Northaw Great Wood (OS 166: TL 282039). Welwyn-Hatfield District Council. Access is from the Ridgeway west of Cuffley.

This is a remnant of the forest that formerly covered a large part of Hertfordshire. There is a car park with a picnic area and toilets. The routes of several footpaths —between $^3/_4$ mile (1200 metres) and $2^1/_4$ miles (3.5 km) — are identified. Muntjac deer, badgers and foxes inhabit the area, and some seventy species of birds have been recorded. A folder about the wood and its wildlife can be obtained on the site.

Paradise Wildlife Park, White Stubbs Lane, Hoddesdon. Telephone: 0992 468001. *Open daily.*

This is a small zoo particularly suitable for children, with a picnic area and varied entertainments.

Rickmansworth Aquadrome, Harefield Road, Rickmansworth. Information from the Council Offices — telephone: 0923 776611.

The Aquadrome is a recreational area of 100 acres (40 hectares) within the Colne Valley Park. Facilities for sailing, water-skiing, watersurfing and model yacht sailing are pre-let to clubs. There are opportunities for lakeside and woodland walks, bird watching and angling, with a barbecue area and picnic tables. Access by car is from Harefield Road (first turn to the right south of Batchworth Bridge over the canal).

Rye House Marsh Reserve, Stanstead Abbots (OS 166: TL 387101). Royal Society for the Protection of Birds. Telephone: 0992 460031. *Open at weekends only.*

The reserve, which adjoins the car park at Rye House, provides opportunities for viewing birds of the marshes and wetlands.

Symondshyde Picnic Area, Hatfield (OS 166: TL 200107). CMS. The wood, with car park and picnic tables, lies west of the road from Stanborough to St Albans. Entrance is from Hammond's Lane.

This is an area mostly of old oak and hornbeam coppice, with some young birch and open grass and heathland. These varied habitats attract a similarly varied wildlife.

Therfield Heath, Royston. Access is from A505 or the Therfield Road.

The heath is an outstanding area of chalk downland with a rich flora, notably the pasque flower and five species of orchid. It is protected as a Site of Special Scientific Interest. Sheep regularly graze here to maintain the grassland, so please keep dogs under control.

Tring Reservoirs National Nature Reserve. Nature Conservancy Council. 1 mile (1.6 km) north of Tring. Car park opposite the Anglers' Retreat public house on B489 road at the north side of Startops End Reservoir.

The four reservoirs were declared a National Nature Reserve in 1955 and a Grade 1 Site of Special Scientific Interest. They were built in 1802-39 to store water for the Grand Junction (now Grand Union) Canal, which reaches a summit nearby. The nature trail, which starts near the Anglers' Retreat, is nearly 2 miles (3 km) long, but this can be shortened to a mile if desired. For most visitors the main interest will be in the birdlife, but trees and marshland flora can also be studied here. The water plants, fish and insects, and the setting amid reedbeds and woodland, attract a great variety of birds at all seasons. Large flocks of ducks winter here, and many other varieties of bird breed on the reservoirs. Hides are provided for the use of visitors.

Ver-Colne Valley Walk. CMS.

This 15 mile (24 km) path, which begins at Redbourn in the north, follows the river Ver and subsequently the Colne downstream through St Albans to Watford. (A northward extension from Redbourn to Flamstead is planned.) There are many opportunities for joining or leaving the route at intermediate points: it is not usually necessary even to plan a route back to your starting point since British Rail runs a convenient service between Watford Junction and St Albans Abbey, with four stations accessible to the path, though the line does not obtrude into the view. Several picnic sites and public houses also lie close to the path. In the vicinity of St Albans the route crosses Verulamium Park (see page 57). Here and at some other points there are spectacular views of the cathedral. The route also passes the ruins of 'Sopwell Nunnery' (see page 86). Much of this walk lies through waterside meadows and some stretches will be very muddy after rain.

Whippendell Woods, Watford. Watford Borough Council. Telephone: 0923 226400, extension 2501.

Whippendell Woods include 200 acres (80 hectares) of woodland (mostly beech, oak and hornbeam) with footpaths, picnic areas and two nature trails starting from the car park in Grove Mill Lane. 55 kinds of birds and 22 kinds of mammal have been identified. The woods can also be reached on foot from Cassiobury Park. A printed guide to the nature trails is available.

Wilbury Hill, Letchworth (OS 166: TL 201326). CMS.

A car park and picnic site just south of the Wilbury Hotel provide a base for a three quarters of an hour walk, starting westward along the hedge behind the Wilbury, then via Cadwell Farm and returning on the Icknield Way.

4
Places of archaeological interest

Arbury Banks, Ashwell (OS 153: TL 262387). The site can be approached from Partridge Hill bridleway, which runs southward from the Newnham Way/Hinxworth Road junction west of Ashwell.

This is an iron age rampart and ditch enclosing a farmstead of 12½ acres (5 hectares). The sites of a circular hut and some other enclosures have been located within the rampart by aerial photography.

The Aubreys, Redbourn (OS 166: TL 095113). Take the B487 west and fork right immediately after passing Redbourn church. After the road passes under the M1, The Aubreys is immediately on the left. A footpath is signposted but there is no easy access.

The circular earthwork of this iron age plateau fort can still be seen although the site is not easy to read at ground level.

Beech Bottom Dyke, St Albans (OS 166: TL 152089).

This ditch runs roughly east-west, crossing the A1081 (St Albans to Harpenden) road about a mile (1.6 km) north of St Peter's church. It can be seen most clearly in the wooded area north of the Ancient Briton public house. A similar short length of dyke known as Devil's Ditch lies 1½ miles (2.5 km) to the west and may have been part of the same system. These dykes belong to the pre-Roman tribal period when in this area the Belgic tribe known as the Catuvellauni had their base in Prae Wood. It is uncertain whether the dykes were defences or merely

Devil's Dyke: iron age defences at Wheathampstead.

The Roman theatre at Verulamium.

territorial boundaries.

Devil's Dyke, Wheathampstead (OS 166: TL 186133). National Trust. Take B653 Marford Road from Wheathampstead. Dyke Lane is on the right-hand side after half a mile (800 metres). Access to the dyke is about 100 yards (90 metres) along, through an iron gate on the left-hand side.

Two earthworks, known as Devil's Dyke and The Slad, may be the defences of an iron age settlement of about 100 acres (40 hectares). This might have been the tribal headquarters of Cassivellaunus, attacked by Julius Caesar in 54 BC (but see also Ravensburgh Castle, page 57). The ditch is an impressive 40 feet (12 metres) deep. The area is thick with bluebells in the spring.

Ermine Street

Roman Ermine Street was constructed at the beginning of the Roman occupation to link London with Lincoln and the north. It runs due north, mostly in a straight line, through Tottenham and Enfield to the crossing of the river Lea at Ware, then on to Royston after an eastward digression towards Braughing. The route is close to that of the present A10, which follows the same straight line for much of the way between Ware and Royston. In the section between Wormley and Hertford Heath the route has long been abandoned and survives as a track through woodland. It is marked on Ordnance Survey maps. Most interesting, though muddy in wet weather, is the mile or so northward from Martin Green on Cock Lane (OS 166: TL 347077) to Goose Green on Lord Street. There are parking places at both ends of this section. For much of the route the agger (embankment) and side ditches can be clearly identified.

Ravensburgh Castle, Hexton (OS 166: TL 099296). The nearest approach is by a footpath running southward from the Barton to Hexton road (B655).

This is an impressive iron age hillfort of about 22 acres (9 hectares), which has been suggested, on the evidence of cultivation, as one of several possible locations for the Catuvellaunian stronghold attacked by Julius Caesar in 54 BC. In heavily wooded country, it is not normally easily visible. A good view can be obtained looking westward from the highest point on the Hexton to Lilley road. It is privately owned, but between February and April visits by parties may be made by prior arrangement. Telephone: 0582 881204.

Therfield Heath, Royston (OS 154: TL 342402).

A cemetery consisting of ten round barrows, including the Five Hills, apparently grouped round a single long barrow, lies on the skyline south of the route of the Icknield Way. It has been attributed to the late neolithic/early bronze age. One mile (1.6 km) to the west an iron age earthwork known as the Mile Ditches runs at right angles to the Icknield Way and on both sides of it, probably one of a series of territorial boundary markers along this route.

Verulamium, St Albans.

The Roman city of Verulamium was a self-governing civilian settlement situated on Watling Street, the road from London to Chester. It was established in the early years of Roman occupation (probably AD 50) and, although devastated during Boudica's rebellion in AD 61, continued to flourish until the end of the Roman era. The site was extensively excavated by Sir Mortimer Wheeler in the early 1930s and more recently by Professors Frere and Manning.

With certain exceptions it is now once more covered by the turf of the civic park and sports pitches on the west side of the river

Welwyn Roman Baths.

Ver. The parish church of St Michael (see page 70) is on the site of the basilica, close to the forum and administrative offices. Opposite is Verulamium Museum (see page 97), with ample car parking nearby. The main features of the site (walls, theatre, hypocaust) are well signposted. At the site labelled 'hypocaust' the mosaic floor of a room in a residential building has been preserved *in situ* to show the method of underfloor heating using ducted hot air. The foundations of the south-east gate, by which Watling Street entered the town from London, are preserved at the far end of the park. Beyond this the wall with its surrounding ditch is well preserved.

The Roman theatre (about AD 150, with later alterations) lies west of the museum, facing on to the old route of Watling Street where it passed through the city. The remains include substantial foundations within the stage area and the layout of gangways and tiered seats which constituted the auditorium.

A theatre of this kind would have been used for stage performances and perhaps animal fights, but not for the spectacular contests characteristic of the larger Roman amphitheatres.

Welwyn Roman Baths, Welwyn (OS 166: TL 235160). Telephone: 0707 271362. Access is from a roundabout on the Welwyn link road, reached from the Hertford Road (A1000).
Open afternoons only, Thursday to Sunday and Bank Holidays.

The bath-house was discovered in the 1960s during archaeological excavation prior to the building of the A1 motorway. It formed part of a third-century farm or villa. The bath-house alone has been preserved *in situ*, in a vault beneath the motorway. The full plan of the building can be viewed from a catwalk and is clearly explained.

The church in the fields at Ayot St Lawrence.

5
Churches

This chapter contains only churches considered to be of outstanding interest. Some other references will be found in chapter 2. The majority of these churches are unlocked during the daytime. Most of the others display the address where a key can be obtained. In the minority of cases where this is not done the key will usually be found at a nearby house.

Aldenham: St John the Baptist.

This is a beautiful church, full of interest. The chancel, tower and Lady Chapel are of the thirteenth century, while the nave and south aisle seem to have been rebuilt in the early fourteenth century and the north aisle is later still. No attempt has been made to match these different building stages: the nave arcades are dissimilar, the two aisles are un-balanced and the chancel is offset from the line of the nave. Most alarmingly, the west-ern arch on the north side of the chancel now hangs without any supporting pillar. The outstanding monument is the double tomb chest of the Crowmer ladies (late fourteenth-century) in the Lady Chapel. The fifteenth-century rood screen is notable for the com-plete preservation (much restored) of its ac-cess stair and loft. Beneath the tower is a fine fourteenth-century coffer made from a 10 foot (3 metre) hollowed-out tree trunk.

Anstey: St George.

St George's is one of the most handsome village churches in the county. The outside view from the south is especially impressive. The church is cruciform, with a Norman tower at its centre. Chancel and transepts were rebuilt in the thirteenth century, possibly with materials from the neighbouring castle whose fortifications were ordered to be demolished in 1218. The nave is somewhat later. Notable features include the Norman font, which has a design of linked mermen, crudely carved, a fine canopied tomb recess in the south trans-ept, and misericords beneath seven stalls in the chancel. The church is rich in medieval graffiti, especially on the eastern respond of the south arcade. The lychgate, probably of the fifteenth century, was adapted in the nine-teenth century to serve as the parish 'cage' or lock-up (see page 83).

Ashwell: St Mary.

The elegant tower is a landmark through-out the area of rolling country where Hert-fordshire, Bedfordshire and Cambridgeshire meet. The whole building is of the fourteenth century. There was no doubt an earlier church but nothing of this survives.

Ashwell's unique treasure is its medieval graffiti, including written inscriptions on three pillars of the south arcade and in the tower, and a series of eight drawings, mostly of churches, on two pillars in the north arcade and inside the tower. Outstanding among these are three Latin inscriptions in the tower relating to the Black Death in 1349 and to the plague and great storm of 1361, and the de-tailed drawing inside the tower of Old St Paul's Cathedral before its spire was de-stroyed by lightning in 1561.

The interior of the church, though high and spacious, is strangely devoid of decoration or significant monuments. In many respects this is a twin of the church at Baldock: Ashwell is a little later in date and a little grander in style, suggesting a rivalry between the two par-ishes.

Ayot St Lawrence: old and new St Lawrence churches.

The ruins of the old church (about 1300) stand in the main street of the village, their dangerous state making it necessary to keep the gate locked. The partial destruction of this building (halted, it is said, by the inter-vention of the bishop) and its replacement by a new church were the work of Sir Lionel Lyde, an eighteenth-century lord of the manor.

The remarkable new church, built in 1778-9 and designed by Nicholas Revett, stands in fields a little beyond the edge of the village. Basically, it is a small rectangular box, standing behind a Greek portico with left- and right-hand colonnades leading to two widely separated open pavilions.

Ayot St Peter: St Peter.

Designed in 1874 by J.P. Seddon in patterned varicoloured brick with a spire and a complex ground plan, attractive enough in itself but incongruous in a rural village setting, St Peter's replaces a previous church which was destroyed by lightning. The Arts and Crafts interior, mainly in red and green, features a ceramic chancel arch, delicate wrought-iron screen and satisfying apse.

Baldock: St Mary.

A fourteenth-century church containing some traces of a thirteenth-century building, St Mary's has many points of similarity to Ashwell, but this church was slightly earlier and was therefore perhaps the pattern, not the copy. The most impressive feature is the full set of fifteenth-century screens, spanning the

The Norman font decorated with mermen at Anstey church.

chancel arch and two equally broad aisles. There are some good brasses, but no other notable monuments.

Bengeo: St Leonard.

St Leonard's has remained substantially unspoilt since it was built early in the twelfth century. It consists of a simple rectangular nave and a chancel with apsidal east end. The overall length is about 70 feet (20 metres). The capitals of the chancel arch are crudely carved, and some wall painting survives on either side. Extensive restoration was undertaken during 1992.

The few changes which have been made in the building are easily recognised and no impediment to understanding its original appearance. The roof, now tiled, would once have been thatched. Some windows have been enlarged; the porch was added in the eighteenth century and the bellcote in the nineteenth. The only real offence is caused by two out-of-scale seventeenth-century monuments in the chancel. A panel in the north wall of the chancel reveals access to a former anchorite's cell.

Benington: St Peter.

This church was built mostly around 1300, with the north chancel chapel added a few years later and the tower not until after 1500. The arrangement of chancel and north chancel chapel is similar to that at Little Munden: in both churches two tomb chests are sheltered beneath adjoining arches in the north wall of the chancel, and in both churches one of these tombs has an elaborately carved ogee canopy. At Benington the occupants of this tomb have not been identified, but it seems to be a century earlier and more primitive in design than the one at Little Munden. Here, however, is a puzzle: the second and later tomb at Benington is believed to be that of Sir Edward de Benstede (died 1432) and his wife Joan (died 1448); and Joan was the sister of Sir Philip Thornbury (died 1456) who occupies the tomb beneath the ogee arch at Little Munden. Perhaps when Philip came to Benington to attend his sister's funeral in 1448 he so admired the adjoining tomb that he had it copied (and improved upon) for his own.

Bishop's Stortford: St Michael.

St Michael's is a large light building of the fifteenth century, rendered with cement in the nineteenth. The nave and aisles have not been significantly altered since they were built: the roofs are original; the windows in the aisles are late Perpendicular in style. Corbels in the nave and aisles are carved to depict apostles, saints, grotesque figures and country people with the tools of their trades. The fine north doorway was inserted in about 1490. The chancel, lengthened in the seventeenth century, was more extensively modified during the nineteenth when the chancel arch was raised and the clerestory added. The original east window is now in the south wall of the chancel.

Three fine timber features are especially worthy of note. The rood screen, contemporary with the main building, has a matching lightness and delicacy; the vaulted canopy added in 1885 seems deliberately intended to prevent it from floating away. The rood itself, which once stood above this screen, was demolished at the Reformation. The beam which supported the rood is believed now to form the top part of the fireplace in the bar of the Boar's Head inn, opposite the church: slots for the rood and attendant figures are still visible. The eighteen choir stalls have elaborately carved misericords beneath their seats: there is a local tradition that they came originally from Old St Paul's Cathedral. The pulpit was made by a local carpenter in 1658: churchwardens' accounts record that he was paid £5.

Braughing: St Mary.

This was one of the minsters or missionary churches in the early period of Christianisation. The size of the present church, which was mainly rebuilt in the early fifteenth century and restored in 1888, still reflects this status, as well as the affluence of Braughing's medieval community. Except for a thirteenth-century lancet window in the chancel, all the window tracery dates from the 1888 restoration. There are some fine monuments, especially to members of the Brograve and Freman families, successive owners of Hamels.

A notable feature of the church is the fine two-storeyed Perpendicular porch, which originally had a priest's room (parvise) on the upper level. The inner doorway to the church is offset to provide room for an access stair or ladder to the upper floor.

Buntingford: St Peter.

Buntingford lies mainly within the parish of Layston, whose church, St Bartholomew, now stands half-ruined and isolated about 1 mile (1.6 km) to the east, accessible from Buntingford via Church Street. It is used only as a cemetery chapel. St Peter's was built in 1614 at the south end of the High Street as a chapel-of-ease for Layston parishioners. The design, brick-built on a Grecian cross plan, was revolutionary for its time and still seems remarkably modern. An existing apse on the south side was heightened in 1899, and there was further extensive re-ordering during the 1980s.

Bygrave: St Margaret.

This remote and unsophisticated rural church has a Norman nave, later chancel and no tower. An appropriately rustic bell-frame is attached to the nave at its west end. The eastern angles of the nave are strengthened with tiles, like the porch at Hinxworth.

. Inside, via a Norman doorway, three features catch the eye: the seventeenth-century pulpit retains its contemporary wrought-iron hourglass stand; the chancel, added in the late fourteenth century, is offset to the south for no obvious reason; some aged poppy-head benches are disposed within the fifteenth-century screen.

Cottered: St John the Baptist.

In this simple, light, aisleless fourteenth-century church a large wall painting of St Christopher of the same date faces the entrance door, where it was rediscovered and restored after having been covered with limewash. A large boulder has been incorporated in the lowest courses of the tower (see also Sawbridgeworth, page 71).

Digswell: St John the Baptist.

This much altered twelfth-century building was successfuly enlarged in 1960-2 by the addition of a new nave, to which the original

Hinxworth parish church with its modest brick chancel.

nave is now in effect a north aisle. The north wall of the old church contains several architectural features of interest. Among the brasses in the sanctuary is that of John Peryent, standard-bearer to King Richard II, and his wife Joan (1415).

East Barnet: St Mary the Virgin.

The nave walls survive from the early Norman church, with three round-headed windows on the north side and north and south doorways. Patterns visible on the outside of the north wall in damp conditions suggest a timber-frame construction. The gallery is believed to have been inserted in 1631. The present chancel, south chapel and tower (originally free-standing) are all of the nineteenth century.

Flamstead: St Leonard.

Here there is a Norman tower and nave, to which aisles were added in the thirteenth century and the chancel and chancel arch in the fourteenth century. When the nave was widened the height of the tower was increased, and it became necessary to strengthen the round-headed and very broad tower arch by inserting a smaller Gothic arch into it. This is clearly visible from within the nave.

A rich series of wall paintings, including a large St Christopher above the north arcade, was revealed in the 1920s. They had been much damaged by the addition of the clerestory in the thirteenth century. The church is also rich in graffiti: notable are three rhyming epitaphs to deceased parishioners, carved on pillars in the nave.

Great Amwell: St John the Baptist.

This Norman church is one of three in Hertfordshire which retain a round-headed Norman chancel arch and an apsidal east end (see also Bengeo and Great Wymondley). The seventeenth-century pulpit is said to have been made from the old sounding board of the pulpit of Old St Paul's Cathedral. The main fascination of this church derives from its magical location, the sloping churchyard precariously overlooking the New River, with yews and cypresses above, willows below (see page 26).

Great Wymondley: St Mary.

St Mary's is one of Hertfordshire's three small Norman churches which have retained an apsidal chancel. Its outer wall has the most beautiful texture, having been built not with flint alone but with a variety of gathered stones. Entry is via a south doorway, with primitive carvings of faces on its capitals and a beautifully patterned tympanum. Characteristically in such a church, a solid wall pierced by a round-headed arch separates nave from chancel. The wooden ceiling of the chancel, like an upturned boat, is perhaps a replacement but no doubt demonstrates the original method of construction. There was formerly a rood loft, reached as usual by a spiral staircase (still intact) within the thickness of the wall. A tower was added in the fifteenth century.

Hemel Hempstead: St Mary.

St Mary's is a large Norman church completed in 1180, and second only to St Albans Abbey for its beauty and architectural interest. The chancel (about 1150) is unique among parish churches in the county in having a vaulted roof. The central tower carries a leaded spire, restored in the 1980s, on round-headed Norman arches. The nave arcades consist of six pairs of similar arches, surmounted (unusually) by a contemporary clerestory. Discreet restoration of the interior in 1880 and about 1980 has not diminished the grandeur of this very fine church.

Hertford: Meeting House, Railway Street (Society of Friends). For access telephone 0992 59411.

Said to be 'the oldest purpose-built Quaker Meeting House in the world to have been in continuous use for worship throughout its existence', the building, which dates from 1669-70, is set back from the street behind a walled courtyard. The main meeting room, with its unique four-tiered platform for 'ministers', is separated from the entrance area by removable partitions. There is a small garden at the rear.

Hinxworth: St Nicholas.

A low tower, a slab-sided castellated nave and a modest chancel looking like a small dinghy being towed along behind, all stand as if in a vast turfed lake, approached by an avenue of trees. The contrast with the interior is startling, for this is a strangely endearing church, characterised not by marble memorials to local gentry but by small, modern tablets which commemorate a clerk-sexton and two bellringers. The primitive lines of the chancel arch suggest local unskilled workmanship.

The distance between the arch and the entry to the rood stair, and the uncertain (apparently altered) route of the stairs point to a significant reconstruction at some early date. The church has some fine brasses.

Hitchin: St Mary.

There was a minster church here at the time of Domesday Book, but the earliest surviving feature is the low twelfth-century tower. The rest of that building seems to have perished in an earthquake in 1298. The fourteenth-century rebuilding reflects the prosperity of that period, derived from the wool trade. Particularly notable features are the two-storeyed porch, the screens between the aisles and the two chapels, and the ceilings throughout the church.

Note also the collection of brasses in the south chancel chapel. Lying uncomfortably on window ledges in the north aisle, whither they have been removed from elsewhere, are the reclining figures of Bernard de Baliol, lord of the manor of Hitchin in the twelfth century, and of Sir Edward de Kendale (died 1373) and his wife Elizabeth, who must once have lain side by side. An old-style ambulatory has been re-created behind the high altar.

Hoddesdon: St Catherine and St Paul.

The first recorded place of worship here was a chapel built in 1336 to serve pilgrims from London to the shrine at Walsingham in Norfolk: St Catherine is the patron saint of pilgrims. A new chapel was built in 1732. Hoddesdon was created a separate parish in 1856 and in 1864-5 the chapel was enlarged to serve as the new parish church, dedicated in 1901 'in the name of St Paul'. The two dedications were merged in 1976. The Victorian red-brick exterior gives no warning of the light and gracious interior, to which the incorporated 1732 chapel contributes an elegant pedimented gallery.

Hunsdon: St Dunstan.

The parish church of Hunsdon lies remote from the village, immediately next to Hunsdon House, which was surrounded by parkland. The house, built in the fifteenth

The tomb of Sir Philip Thornbury (about 1456) at Little Munden.

century, became a residence of Henry VIII and a nursery for his children. Only a quarter of that great mansion survives in the present building. Slight traces of fourteenth-century work remain in the church. Most of the earliest features are of the fifteenth century: the west tower, the fine north porch and the rood screen, of which only the lowest section remains. A handsome new screen was erected in the seventeenth century across the entrance to the newly built brick south chapel, within which are some Jacobean box pews and the magnificent alabaster monument to Sir John Carey (died 1617) and his wife.

Kelshall: St Faith.

This building of about 1400 (restored 1870) has two outstanding features. The lower part of the original rood screen has survived, its four panels containing portraits of St Edmund, St Edward the Confessor and two bishops. These were cleaned in 1979, and their former colours revealed. At the west end of the north

aisle is a narrow niche, 12 feet (3.6 metres) high, perhaps built to accommodate a processional cross. Similar 'cross lockers' have been reported in Suffolk churches and at St Sepulchre's, Northampton.

Kings Langley: All Saints.

In this handsome fifteenth-century church with wide aisles and chapels the main points of interest are the magnificent early seventeenth-century carved chanticleer pulpit and the north chapel. This contains two tomb chests: that of Edmund of Langley, a son of Edward III (and the first Duke of York); and, more modest, that of Sir Ralph Verney, son of a Lord Mayor of London (died 1528).

King's Walden: St Mary.

The present building is mainly of the twelfth century. As commonly happened, the height of the nave was increased, and a clerestory added, in the fifteenth century. This is one of several churches in the county to which a brick chapel has been added, in this case by William Hale in 1687. The church contains an outstanding piece of medieval graffiti: the head of a jester (?) playing a shawm, scratched on the pillar by the belfry door. There is a good south window by William Morris (1867).

Knebworth: St Martin.

St Martin's, designed by Sir Edwin Lutyens, was built in two phases: by Lutyens (1914-15) and by Sir Albert Richardson (1963-4). Its remarkable interior, clean, bright and spacious, is dominated by two gigantic Tuscan columns placed on the centre line of the two short transepts. Their size has been enhanced by the later addition nearby of two self-conscious spirals of miniature organ pipes, flanking a similarly matching pair of pulpit-lecterns. A shell-like reredos provides a rather theatrical backcloth. The two western bays of the nave, the work of Sir Albert Richardson, again respect the scale of the dominant columns by the use of low Moorish arches with plain walls above, to separate the two aisles from the nave. The Mediterranean influences so evident inside the church are continued outside in the dramatically deep roof eaves.

Little Gaddesden: St Peter and St Paul.

This is a modest church, seemingly relegated to a remote corner of the village. The tower and north side of the nave are probably fifteenth-century, but the rest of the building is mainly Victorian. There are some fine memorials, notably those of the Bridgewater family of Ashridge, including a wall monument, previously at St Martin's in the Fields, London, commemorating Elizabeth Dutton who died in 1611 at the age of sixteen. The hexagonal pulpit has been embellished by the insertion of small delicately coloured figures of angels into three niches on each of its sides, the work of Mary Watts, wife of the artist G. F. Watts.

Little Hadham: St Cecilia.

The church is reached by narrow Church End Lane on the north side of the A120. It is far from the village centre, but close to Hadham Hall, once one of the county's most noble residences. The church is unusual in both its plan and its furnishing. The date is about 1400, but the nave walls may be older. There is an unusual brick-built north transept or alcove of later date, contained within a broad four-centred arch. The elegant but unsophisticated screen and the timber porch are of the fifteenth century. Box pews face towards a three-decker pulpit opposite the transept.

Little Hormead: St Mary.

St Mary's is a small, isolated, unspoiled Norman church, which is further distinguished by the magnificent north door with its twelfth-century iron decoration. It merits a very considerable detour. Even the roof timbers have been judged to be original. The door was removed in 1985 to be included in the exhibition of Romanesque art at the Hayward Gallery in London, and at that time it was carefully restored.

Little Munden: All Saints.

The church stands in an isolated position midway between Dane End and Green End, with only the school and rectory nearby. The twelfth-century date of the main building is revealed by two details: the cable moulding on the capitals of the first archway between

nave and aisle, and a round-headed doorway in the south wall of the chancel. The nave was re-roofed in the fourteenth century (two king posts) when the north aisle was added.

Between the chancel and the Lady Chapel stand two fine tombs bearing the reclining figures of Sir John Thornbury (died 1396) and of his son Sir Philip Thornbury (died about 1456), each with his wife. The later of these tombs stands beneath a magnificent ogee arch. Benington has a similar monument of a century earlier which may have been a model for this one.

Meesden: St Mary.

This church is a little treasure hidden in a wood, 1/2 mile (800 metres) east of the village. (A map is needed to find it.) The location is magical, accessible from the road only by an unmade track. The church is a delight in itself, with twelfth-century nave, solid two-bay arcades leading to rudimentary transepts (thirteenth-century, rebuilt 1877), and a brick porch of about 1530. The real gem, however, is the mosaic tile pavement in front of the altar, attributed to the first quarter of the fourteenth century.

Monken Hadley: St Mary.

The manor was held at one time by the monks of Walden Abbey, Essex, hence the name of the parish. The present church, built in 1494, has some interesting architectural features, including the use of four-centred arches in the arcades, absence of a chancel arch, and the existence of squints from both north and south aisles towards the altar. There are many small brasses, mostly of the sixteenth century, and some good seventeenth-century monuments. The church is especially notable, however, for the eighteenth-century copper beacon which still stands on top of the tower, perhaps the only one remaining in Britain.

Much Hadham: St Andrew.

The present building was begun in 1225. Its earliest feature is the oak door to the left of the altar, moved from some other position in the church. Two tall-backed oak seats are probably survivors from a three-seat fourteenth-century sedilia. Work continued on the building until about 1450: the handsome porch was probably the final touch. Very little has changed since the Reformation.

The sculptor Henry Moore, a local resident, contributed the two head stops, a king and a queen, on either side of the west door.

Northchurch: St Mary.

It is difficult to believe that this is basically a Saxon church. It stands beside the busy A41 in an urban setting on the outskirts of Berkhamsted. But Berkhamsted is the new-comer, and this was the original settlement in the area. The original Saxon church has be-come the present nave, the south and west walls of which are substantially original. The thickening of the wall at the west end has been interpreted as an indication that there was formerly a separate west chamber, prob-ably the priest's room. The Saxon church may have had a small chancel, which would have occupied the site of the present central tower. That tower and the present chancel were built in the thirteenth century, the tower

One of the head stops by Henry Moore at Much Hadham church.

needing to be strengthened in the fifteenth century. The north aisle, vestries and porch were all added in 1881.

A brass memorial on the south wall com-memorates Peter the Wild Boy, who is buried just outside the porch. Peter was found in 1725, living wild in a wood near Hanover in Germany. He was brought to England at the instigation of the royal family and eventually committed to the care of a farmer at Haxter's End, subsequently at Broadway Farm, in this parish. He died in 1785 at the estimated age of 75.

Offley: St Mary Magdalene.

At first glance this is a conventional medi-eval church with a thirteenth-century nave, aisles with windows renewed in the four-teenth century, and a later tower. However, the chancel, beyond a restyled round-headed arch, was largely rebuilt in about 1777, with an apsidal east end containing a stuccoed canopy and hanging draperies (see also St Paul's Walden, refurbished 1727). The effect is not unpleasing, though seriously out of place here. The benefactor responsible was Sir Thomas Salusbury (died 1773), uncle to Mrs Thrale, the friend of Dr Johnson. An overbearing monument to Sir Thomas and his wife, by Nollekens, dominates the south side of the chancel, emphasising its true function as a Salusbury memorial chapel.

Oxhey: Chapel.

Oxhey Chapel comes as a great shock. Built in chequered flint and brick, with stone quoins and a pitched roof, it stands in the middle of a housing estate, ½ mile (800 metres) west of Carpenders Park railway station, next door to All Saints, a gaunt modern church. The chapel itself, demure in its outside appearance, was built in 1612 by Sir James Altham, adjoining his great house St Cleeres, later Oxhey Place. It seats forty, in two double rows of seats facing a central aisle. The building is darkly wainscoted and is now dominated by a heavy reredos inserted in about 1690, possibly re-moved from Oxhey Place when it was demol-ished in 1688. (A second Oxhey Place was burned down in 1955.) A delicately carved font, also of about 1690, is perhaps the chapel's finest possession.

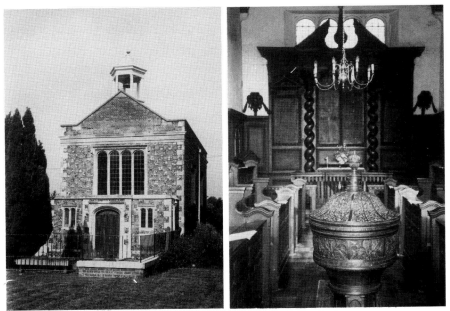

Oxhey Chapel: the exterior (left), and (right) the interior showing the font.

Pirton: St Mary.

St Mary's was originally a cruciform church with a wide nave and massive central tower. It was built within the precincts of the castle (whose earthen mound, Toot Hill, survives beside the churchyard) in about 1100. The tower, however, proved to be unstable: in the thirteenth century the south arch collapsed, severely damaging the south transept, and a few years later the north arch also collapsed and demolished much of the tower and the north transept. Solid walls were built to strengthen the tower and close off the remains of the transepts, and they remained there until the nineteenth century.

By that time the east-west line of the church was divided by partitions into three sections: services were held in the nave, the tower was reserved for the bellringers, and the chancel became a Sunday school. The building was in a very poor condition. In 1876 the tower was completely dismantled and rebuilt, and in 1883 the nave was restored and re-roofed. The building of a new south transept was completed in 1914 as a great do-it-yourself project involving the whole village. The architectural history of Pirton church is of great interest but the present furniture and fittings are mostly of the twentieth century.

Royston: St John the Baptist.

As long as its priory existed, Royston was not constituted an ecclesiastical parish. It fell within several of the rural parishes (Barkway and Therfield on the Hertfordshire side), though the priory church would have been available to the residents for certain purposes. When the priory was demolished in 1537 this facility ceased, and three years later an Act of Parliament established a new parish of Royston and allowed the townspeople to purchase the priory church as their parish church. By that time the building had been seriously vandalised, and considerable renovation was needed. Further renovation and extension were undertaken in the nineteenth century.

What remains today is mainly the former chancel of the priory church. On the north side of the present chancel step, behind the pulpit, is a complete thirteenth-century lancet window and part of another. These are the remains of the triple window which existed when this was the outside wall of the priory. Facing them across the church is the upper

A triple window of the former priory church at Royston, cut into by a later arcade.

part of a matching triple window on the south side. The lower part of this south-side window was destroyed when arcades were inserted in the present church, probably in the seventeenth or eighteenth century. (In 1891 the former east window, behind the altar, was replaced by an inept copy of one of these triple lancets.) Most of the present chancel is nineteenth-century work, as is the tower at the west end. Outside the west door, the wall on the left (south) side is the south wall of the former nave.

St Albans: Cathedral and Abbey Church of St Alban.

The hill above the river Ver, where St Alban was martyred, probably during the third century, was later the site of a Benedictine abbey, said to have been founded by the Saxon King Offa of Mercia, about AD 793. Little more is known of it during the Saxon period. The abbey church, now the cathedral, was the dominant structure within the abbey complex, especially after its rebuilding in the eleventh century. A little to the westward, and still surviving, was the great gateway, built in 1360. This became a focus for attack during the Peasants' Revolt in 1381. After the dissolution of monastic buildings it was used as a prison until 1870, when the grammar school moved here from the Lady Chapel

of the abbey church. The gateway is still part of St Albans School. By the time of the abbey's dissolution in 1539 its buildings and courtyards covered most of the open space which now lies between the cathedral and the river. All were demolished. Remains of the arcading of the fourteenth-century cloister can still be seen in the outside south wall of the nave. The abbey church was purchased by the townspeople as their parish church, and the former parish church (St Andrew's), which adjoined the north wall of the nave, was demolished in its stead.

The abbey church was completely rebuilt by the first Norman abbot, Paul of Caen, in the eleventh century. His building materials included a great deal of Roman brick and tile removed from the ruins of nearby Verulamium: they are particularly evident in the tower and on the south side of the nave. Paul's architect also incorporated some Saxon baluster shafts probably from the earlier church, high up in the east wall of the transepts. In about 1200 the nave was extended westward by three bays, and a new west front added. The east end was largely rebuilt, and the Lady Chapel added, between 1250 and 1320. In 1323 five bays on the south side of the nave, just west of the later screen, collapsed and had to be rebuilt, as can still be detected. The reredos behind the high altar was completed in 1484, but the figures which filled its niches were destroyed at the Reformation and not restored until the 1890s.

By 1870 it became clear that the church was in a state of near collapse: the west front was already a ruin. Only minor repairs could be undertaken with the limited funds available. The solution eventually adopted was to accept an offer by the future Lord Grimthorpe, a wealthy amateur architect, to undertake the restoration of the building at his own expense, provided that he was given a free hand. As a result the building was saved, but sadly compromised: the most notable casualty was the west front, which is now entirely Grimthorpe's Victorian creation. His portrait, as St Matthew, is carved above the doors in the west porch. Ironically it was during these developments that the new see of St Albans was created in 1877, and the former abbey church became a cathedral.

The most striking feature of the nave is the series of wall paintings from the thirteenth and fourteenth centuries which decorate five of the piers on the north side. These paintings were discovered in 1863 after being hidden under whitewash for many years, as a result of which most of their surface colour has been lost. They include representations of the Crucifixion, scenes from the life of the Virgin, and portraits of saints. Several other paintings occur elsewhere in the abbey. The painted ceiling over the east end of the nave survives from the fifteenth century. The round-headed Norman arches of the central crossing beneath the tower are part of the original eleventh-century building.

A new shrine, built in about 1300 to contain the relics of St Alban, was demolished at the Reformation, but buried fragments found during building work in 1872 have been reassembled in their original position in the

St Albans Cathedral: the round-headed arches of the Norman nave with painted decoration.

'Saint's Chapel' behind the high altar. The shrine has been reconstructed and was rededicated in 1993. This was the goal of the pilgrims who thronged to the abbey in the middle ages. They would have entered the abbey church by a door in the north transept, then in a long queue they followed the ambulatory to the shrine. Here they would light and erect their candles and kneel in prayer. Overlooking the shrine is a timber watching chamber (about 1400) from which monks kept constant watch over the shrine.

The Lady Chapel, farther to the east, was built about 1400. After the Dissolution it became the first home of the grammar school. During that period it was separated from the rest of the church by a public walled passage, for which openings were constructed in the north and south walls. A chapter house, opened in 1982, adjoining the south transept incorporates refreshment room, shop and lavatories for visitors.

St Albans: St Michael.

In spite of the uncharacteristic thickness of its walls, this is basically a simple rectangular Saxon church. Aisles were added in the twelfth century, the nave was heightened and part of the south aisle extended to form a Lady Chapel. Considerable further alteration took place in the nineteenth century. Roman materials from Verulamium (within which this church is situated) were used in the construction of the Saxon building. Visible Saxon work includes the north doorway into the chancel and the quoins (of Roman brick) at the east corners of the nave. Against the north wall of the chancel stands the magnificent statue of Sir Francis Bacon of Gorhambury (see page 75) asleep in his chair, carved by an unknown sculptor soon after his death in 1626.

St Albans: St Stephen.

Some Saxon work survives in an early Norman building. Roman materials from Verulamium have been used in the construction. Quoins embedded in the west wall indicate the dimensions of the Saxon nave. In the north wall a narrow round-headed Saxon window has been cut into by an early Norman arch, later filled in. Nearby a later pointed arch seems to have given access from the nave to a north aisle, now demolished.

St Ippollitts: St Ippolyts.

The most interesting features about this church are its site and its dedication. It stands on a considerable bluff with extensive views westward, encouraging thoughts of a previous pagan use of the site. Hippolytus was the name of a minor deity in classical Greek mythology, and also of two medieval Christian saints. One of these, like the Greek Hippolytus, was supposedly dragged to his death by wild horses. The reason for the dedication of this church to St Hippolytus is not known, but there does seem to have been a cult associated with horses at St Ippollitts. John Norden wrote in 1598 that '… all passengers by that way on horsebacke thought themselves bound to bring their steedes into the church, even up to the high aulter … where a priest continually attended …' Another local tradition has it that the Knights Templar from nearby Temple Dinsley would ride over to St Ippollitts for a blessing before leaving for the crusades, and visitors are still shown a pillar in the south aisle bearing crosses supposedly cut with their swords as they left.

St Paul's Walden: All Saints.

The plan, comprising chancel, nave and south aisle, was already established by the early fourteenth century. A Lady Chapel was added at the east end of the south aisle in about 1519: to the right of its arched entrance can be seen traces of the former east window of the aisle. The most notable change has taken place in the chancel, which was 'repaired and beautified' by the lord of the manor, Edward Gilbert, in 1727 (see also Offley, refurbished 1777). He added a vaulted ceiling and stuccoed wall decoration, and inserted into the reshaped chancel arch a flamboyant screen which is now painted in pastel green. From the nave the shadow of the original Gothic arch can still be seen.

Sandon: All Saints.

The church is mainly of the fourteenth century; benches survive mostly from the fifteenth. The tower was ponderously supported with brick buttresses in the seventeenth century. Main points of interest are the Easter sepulchre (small but with fine mouldings) in the chancel, the magnificent Fitz Geffery brass (1480) below the chancel step and a handsome Jacobean pulpit.

Sandridge: St Leonard.

A church is known to have been dedicated here about 1119, and extensively rebuilt about 1400. There has been a great deal of later restoration. The tower and west end were rebuilt in 1886 when an earlier tower proved to be unsafe. The chancel walls incorporate some Roman brick, which is used also in the curious chancel arch and stone rood screen. The arch may have survived from the Norman church, the screen from 1400. The circular font is another Roman feature. There are medieval tiles in the chancel.

Sarratt: Holy Cross.

This is basically a small twelfth-century church, consisting of a short nave with north and south transepts, and a chancel which would originally have had an apse. The chancel, however, has twice been extended eastwards. The north and south aisles (and hence the westernmost pair of 'Norman' arches) were not added until 1865. These alterations have produced an extremely complex ground plan. The tower is probably of the fifteenth century, with a later upper stage which includes a feature unique in Hertfordshire, a 'saddleback' or gabled roof.

Sawbridgeworth: Great St Mary.

The designation 'great', well merited by the size of this church, is said merely to distinguish it from 'little' St Mary at nearby Gilston. The puddingstone built into the south wall of the tower (see also Cottered) is sometimes said to indicate a former pagan use of the site. The oldest part of the present building is believed to be the arch from chancel to south chapel, about 1300.

The church is renowned for its collection of brasses of the Leventhorpe, Joscelyn and Chauncy families: the much reproduced brass of John Leventhorpe (died 1435) and his wife Katherine is outstanding. All are well displayed and annotated for the information of visitors.

Standon: St Mary.

This extraordinary and impressive building stands on rising ground overlooking the curve of the main street. The massive fifteenth-century west porch provides a suitable introduction. Inside, the church follows the lie of the land, rising steadily from west to east. Both nave and chancel slope upward from the west door, and there are eight steps from nave to chancel, five from chancel to sanctuary. The chancel was built in the early thirteenth century, the nave perhaps a hundred years later but rebuilt in the nineteenth century. The fifteenth-century bell tower, which stands beside the east end of the south aisle, is the only detached tower in the county. Notable memorials inside the church include wall monuments to Sir Ralph and Sir Thomas Sadleir (1587 and 1606), and the beautiful brasses of John Field and his son (1477).

Stanstead Abbots: St James.

This, the former parish church, is now used only occasionally and since 1977 has been in the care of the Redundant Churches Fund. It is remote from the village on the road to Roydon. The building is mainly of the fifteenth century, virtually unspoilt and with its solid original timber porch. A north chancel chapel was added in brick in 1577. Inside, the church retains the style of the eighteenth century, with whitewashed walls, a full set of high box pews and a magnificent three-decker pulpit. Painted texts adorn the walls above the altar and within the chapel. There are some good brasses and monuments. This church is the best example of its period in the county.

Stevenage: St Nicholas.

The setting of this church is interesting (see page 42) and attractive, and the building with its elegant spire is handsomely proportioned. Aesthetically and historically, however, the interior is disappointing: the comprehensive painting of walls and stonework (including the lower part of the font) has destroyed a lot of its detail and texture. The tower, the oldest surviving part of the building, is of the twelfth century. The body of the church seems to have been rebuilt in the thirteenth century, with the arcades further renewed a century or

Throcking church.

so later. There is no chancel arch: the arcades continue for two bays beyond the screens. There are misericords beneath six of the choir seats. The thirteenth-century font retains its (apparently cut-down) fifteenth-century wooden cover.

Throcking: Holy Trinity.

The most striking feature is the tower, thirteenth-century flint in its lower stages but with the upper stage rebuilt in brick in 1660, with a corbelled stair turret: all top-heavy and rather undignified. The simple aisleless nave has Elwes family memorials by Rysbrack and Nollekens, and a superabundance of consecration crosses.

Tring: St Peter and St Paul.

As so often happens, a thirteenth-century lancet window survives in the north wall of the chancel to provide evidence that this is the oldest surviving part of the church. The tower arch is of the early fourteenth century, and the rest of the building mainly of the fifteenth,

much restored in the nineteenth. The entrance via the south porch is dominated by a massive memorial to Sir William Gore (died 1707) of Tring Park, sometime Lord Mayor of London. His effigy's thumb, broken off soon after the monument was erected, was discovered in a pond over a hundred years later and restored to him.

Once one steps inside, the nave appears light and spacious. Its most interesting decorative features are the carved stone corbels on the two arcades. The painting above the chancel arch dates only from 1899. The battlemented exterior of the church is impressive, but here also the gargoyles and carved heads are of the late nineteenth century. When walking down to view the gatehouse east of the church, note the churchyard wall with its capping bricks carefully carved in an ogee shape.

Walkern: St Mary.

St Mary's is situated at the north end of the village, close to a ford over the river Beane. A Norman doorway gives access to the south aisle added in the twelfth century, but at heart this is a Saxon church. Beyond the aisle, two round-headed arches were cut through the original Saxon outer wall in Norman times. High on the outside of this wall is a primitive carved figure which no doubt represents Christ on the cross. It is probably in its original position above the Saxon entrance door. The single decorated impost below is probably also in its original position on the right-hand side of the Saxon doorway. The area of the Saxon church would have been that of the present nave. The church contains a fine effigy of a thirteenth-century knight, carved in Purbeck marble.

Wallington: St Mary.

This is a complete fifteenth-century church save for the chancel which was rebuilt in 1864. The north chancel chapel seems to be a rather clumsy but near contemporary addition, originally with a double-pitched roof. Large plain glass windows bring light and a sense of spaciousness to the nave. Most notable is the survival of the original rustic-style benches, less sophisticated than those at Sandon. George Orwell (Eric Blair) (see page

105) was married here in 1936.

Waterford: St Michael and All Angels.

This little church was built in 1871-2 by Robert Abel Smith, at the entrance to his estate at Goldings. At that time Waterford was part of Bengeo. It became a separate parish only in 1909 and this its parish church. Externally the building is undistinguished; inside it is a treasure-house of the church arts of its period. There is a handsome Walker organ, mosaic decoration in the chancel by Powell and Sons, and above all a display of stained glass from the William Morris Company which includes designs by Morris, Burne-Jones, Madox Brown and Philip Webb. Nevertheless, a late addition, the St Cecilia window by Carl Parsons, may prove to be the most memorable. This magnificent church should on no account be missed.

Weston: Holy Trinity.

The central crossing with its four round-headed arches comprises the lower part of the Norman tower, which survives intact. The capitals of the piers show a rare variety in their primitive carved decoration. Much of the Norman north transept is also preserved, with a blocked arch and two original windows. There is much of interest too in the fourteenth-century nave, with its original clerestory (now looking into a heightened south aisle) and a fine collection of grotesque corbels supporting the roof. The chancel, rebuilt in 1840 in brick, with an ornate hammerbeam roof, contrasts strangely with the medieval austerity.

Just inside the churchyard gate two stones mark the supposed grave of the legendary Jack O'Legs, a medieval giant who lived, like Robin Hood, in nearby woodland and plundered the rich to feed the poor. When eventually caught in Baldock and about to be hanged he made the customary request to be allowed to shoot an arrow to determine his place of burial: it landed improbably in Weston churchyard.

Wheathampstead: St Helen.

In Norman times this building would have consisted of a nave (as at present, but without aisles) and an apse which extended only half-way along the present chancel. There seems to be Saxon work in the south wall of the south transept, which must therefore have survived from an earlier building. The chancel was extended to its present length in about 1230, and the great crossing tower was probably built by 1300. There followed the south aisle, porch and transepts, all in the fourteenth century, and the north aisle a little later. The canopied piscina on the south side of the sanctuary is an unusual and attractive feature, probably fifteenth-century. The total effect is impressive both in concept and in quality of execution.

As usual, extensive restoration was needed in Victorian times, when a deliberate attempt was made to return the building to its medieval glory. The strange shape of the spire owes something to this restoration. The church contains some fine monuments, including recumbent effigies of Sir John Brocket (died 1558) and his wife in the south transept, and in the north transept an unidentified Garrard memorial of about 1630.

Wyddial: St Giles.

The church dates from the fourteenth century, the north aisle and chapel being added in 1532. They are built entirely of brick, including the three-bay arcade between aisle and nave. Seventeenth-century screens separate the chapel from nave and chancel. Other modification occurred mainly in the nineteenth century. Two windows on the north side each contain four panels of Flemish stained glass of the sixteenth century.

6
Houses and gardens

Ashridge House, Berkhamsted HP4 1NS. Telephone: 044284 3491.
Gardens open Saturday and Sunday afternoons, April to October.

The story of Ashridge begins in 1283, when a monastery was founded here to accommodate the 'College of Bonhommes', and to have the care of a precious relic, a phial supposedly containing the blood of Christ. This brought pilgrims and prosperity to Ashridge until the monastery, like all others, was dissolved in 1539 and the property surrendered to the Crown. It was bequeathed by Henry VIII to his son, Edward VI, who allowed his half-sister Elizabeth to live there. It was acquired in 1604 by the Egerton family, whose later generations included Lords Bridgewater and Brownlow. They remained here until 1921.

By 1800 the old buildings were seriously dilapidated. Rebuilding, put in hand by the seventh Earl of Bridgewater, was undertaken by the Wyatts during the period 1808-21. They created a magnificent neo-Gothic structure, dominated by a massive staircase tower and the elegant spire of the chapel. Of the former monastic buildings, only a barn (much altered), a crypt beneath the main block and a well survive. The house is now a management college.

The lovely natural setting of the house is enhanced by the extensive gardens, which near the house are broken up into several smaller gardens, such as the circular rose garden, the monks' garden and the flint-lined grotto. It all looks particularly splendid in June when the rhododendrons are in bloom.

Benington Lordship Gardens, Benington, near Stevenage SG2 7BS. Telephone: 043885 668.
Gardens open during the summer, Wednesdays, Sundays and Bank Holidays, in the afternoon only.

At the time of Domesday Book Benington was the principal manor of Peter de Valognes. His castle was demolished in 1212; only the dry moat and vestiges of flint walls survive. A large Georgian house now occupies part of the site. In 1832 an impressive folly consisting of entrance gateway and summerhouse was built on the basis of the old walls. The grounds include splendid gardens.

Capel Manor Gardens, Bullsmoor Lane (A105), Enfield, Middlesex (OS 166; TQ 345996). Telephone: 0992 763849.
Open daily (excluding weekends from November to March).

The gardens lie about a mile (1.6 km) south of the Capel Manor Educational Farm (see page 50) on the south side of the M25 and actually in the London Borough of Enfield. They can be reached from the A10 by turning west at the first traffic lights south of the M25 crossing, Junction 25. (The educational farm can be reached from the gardens by a minor road, Bulls Cross Ride, which crosses the M25 west of the A10. A map is provided on admission to the gardens.)

The manor site of some 30 acres (12 hectares) is divided into a large number of smaller gardens, providing a reference collection of examples and ideas for gardeners of every kind. Included are the National Gardening Centre, and the Consumer Association ('Gardening from *Which?*') demonstration and theme gardens.

Cheslyn Gardens, Nascot Wood Road, Watford. Telephone: 0923 226400, extension 2501. Watford Borough Council.

These are gardens of 3½ acres (1.4 hectares) comprising a woodland area and formal garden, including rock garden and aviary. Designed for year-round interest, the gardens contain many rare plants. Spring features include bulbs, wild bluebells, rhododendrons and azaleas.

Gardens of the Rose, Chiswell Green, St Albans AL2 3NR. Telephone: 0727 50461. Royal National Rose Society.
Open daily during the summer.

The Royal National Rose Society is Britain's oldest and largest specialist plant society and its gardens contain an internationally famous collection of old, modern and future garden roses. There are some thirty thousand rose plants in over seventeen hundred varieties displayed with many companion plants.

Gorhambury, St Albans. Telephone: 0727 54051. The house lies west of the A414, up a private drive beside the Roman theatre. *Open only on Thursdays.*

The present house, the home of Lord and Lady Verulam, was built about 1784. It is raised on a plinth and reached by a flight of broad steps via a projecting Corinthian portico. Principal interior features are the magnificent great hall and some chimney pieces attributed to Piranesi. The unrivalled collection of mainly family portraits begins with Edward Grimston (1446) by Peter Christus, the earliest English portrait whose date, artist and sitter are all fully identified.

This is the third manor house to be built in Gorhambury Park. Of the earliest (twelfth-century) no trace remains. The second house, built for Sir Nicholas Bacon in 1563 and subsequently the home of his son Sir Francis, was mostly demolished in 1787, leaving only the ruin still visible from the house windows. When Sir Francis died in 1626 Gorhambury passed to his secretary, Sir Thomas Meautys, whose widow, Anne, married Sir Harbottle Grimston. However, Anne had only a life interest in the property, which was therefore purchased by her husband from the Meautys family in 1652. The property has since remained in the Grimston family.

Hatfield House, Hatfield AL9 5NF. Telephone: 0707 262823. Hatfield House can be approached through gates opposite the rail-

Hatfield House from the south.

way station (this is the entrance for cars, which can park near the house) or through the old gatehouse at the top of Fore Street.

Open from 25th March until second Sunday in October. House, Tuesday to Saturday afternoons, guided tours only; Sunday afternoons and Bank Holiday Mondays, no guided tours; closed other Mondays. Park and gardens open daily during the above period except Good Friday.

The Old Palace on this site, completed in 1496 and formerly owned by the Bishops of Ely, became Crown property in 1538 and was used by Henry VIII mainly as a nursery for his children. During Mary's reign her sister Elizabeth was virtually a prisoner here and is said to have been sitting beneath an oak tree in the park when she received news of Mary's death and her accession. (The very tree, which still stood in the park until 1978, is now exhibited in one of the gift shops of Hatfield House.)

When James I inherited the property he proposed to his chief minister, Robert Cecil, first Earl of Salisbury, an exchange between this and Cecil's own house, Theobalds near Cheshunt, to which he had taken a liking. Cecil took possession of the Old Palace and demolished all but the western range of the building, to make room for a new house. The western range containing the banqueting hall still stands and is used for 'Elizabethan banquets'.

The new house, begun in 1608, was not completed until 1612. Cecil, who died in that year, hardly lived here, but it has been the home of his descendants ever since. It remains one of the great houses of England and is by far the most eminent in Hertfordshire. The plan follows the E-shape characteristic of the late sixteenth century. The main hall with its service doors also follows an earlier tradition. The elaborate south front, which faces the great gates and the road from London, was designed to be the principal entrance: the original open colonnade on the ground floor was enclosed in the nineteenth century to provide a sheltered passage and to house a collection of armour, salvaged from the Spanish Armada. The entrance to the house is now on the north side.

In the park nature trails lead through woodlands and beside a lake, and there are picnic areas. The gardens are being re-created in the seventeenth-century manner, in sympathy with the house. As well as the formal gardens, there are knot, scented and wilderness gardens.

Knebworth House and Country Park, Knebworth SG3 6PY. Telephone: 0438 812661. There is direct access from A1(M) at Junction 7, the South Stevenage exit.
Open from Easter to the end of September, but check days and times.

The spectacular high Gothic appearance of Knebworth House is the creation of Sir Edward Bulwer-Lytton, the Victorian statesman and novelist, in the nineteenth century. It has been the home of the Lyttons since 1490 and inside there survives one range of a courtyard house of about 1500, including the still magnificent great hall, which was transformed into a Jacobean banqueting hall. This is where Dickens took part in amateur theatricals during a visit in 1850 (page 102). The gardens were designed by Sir Edwin Lutyens and include a herb garden by Gertrude Jekyll.

The park aims for a wide popular appeal. It contains herds of red and sika deer and provides countryside activities including horse riding, the Adventure Playground with Fort Knebworth and a miniature railway. Two good timber-framed barns moved from elsewhere serve as restaurants. Close to the house is the parish church (St Mary and St Thomas), Norman in origin with a round-headed chancel arch. It contains the Lytton Chapel (sixteenth-century) with a collection of family memorials.

Moor Park Mansion, Rickmansworth WD3 1QN. Telephone: 0923 776611, extension 125. Three Rivers District Council.
Open Mondays to Fridays, mornings and afternoons, and Saturday mornings; closed Sundays and Bank Holidays.

The magnificent mansion of Moor Park lies south of the canal at Batchworth. (Once across the bridge bear left into Moor Lane; the entrance to the drive is then immediately on the right.) The mansion is owned by the district council but leased to the Moor Park Golf Club as their clubhouse.

Moor Park Mansion, built with profits from the South Sea Bubble.

The property was purchased in 1720 by Benjamin Styles out of his vast profits from the South Sea Bubble. An existing house, built in the sixteenth century by the Earl of Bedford, provided the basis for a virtually new building in the Palladian style, mainly the work of Sir James Thornhill. The cubical entrance hall is decorated in the most lavish style, with painted walls and ceiling. The adjoining dining room, once the ballroom, has a ceiling attributed in part to Robert Adam, who also designed the Batchworth Heath entrance gateway.

The mansion and estate passed through many hands until in 1923 the golf courses were laid out and the mansion became a country club. The estate was purchased by the Rickmansworth Urban District Council in 1937.

Piccotts End Medieval Wall Paintings, near Hemel Hempstead.

At Piccotts End, 1 mile (1.6 km) north of Hemel Hempstead, is a five-gabled timber-framed building of the fifteenth century, which until the 1950s was occupied as a number of separate cottages. In 1953 it was discovered that an entire upper wall in one of these cottages was covered with medieval wall paintings, beneath six layers of wallpaper. This painting continued down to ground level in what had originally been an open hall. These paintings, of religious subjects, have been dated to about 1500, but in another upper room painted decoration of the late sixteenth century has since been found.

It is thought that the building was originally a hospice serving pilgrims bound for the monastery of the Bonhommes at Ashridge. The building became a private house after the Reformation, and for six years after 1827 it was the county's first cottage hospital. The wall paintings are not at present accessible to the public.

St Paul's Waldenbury, St Paul's Walden, Hitchin.
Gardens open on occasional Sundays.

The Bury in St Paul's Walden lies on the west side of the road from Whitwell to Hitchin (B651). It is the home of the Bowes Lyon family and was the childhood home of Queen Elizabeth the Queen Mother. The house, mostly rebuilt in 1887, is not open to the public. The 40 acres (16 hectares) of formal woodland garden were laid out about 1730 and the original concept incorporating temples, statues and vistas has not been changed.

Shaw's Corner, Ayot St Lawrence.

Shaw's Corner, Ayot St Lawrence, Welwyn AL6 9BX.   Telephone: 0438 820307. National Trust.
Open April to October, afternoons, Wednesday to Sunday and Bank Holidays.   Closed Mondays and Tuesdays.

This was the home of George Bernard Shaw from 1906 until his death in 1950 (see page 106).

Berkhamsted Castle.

7
Other historic buildings and ruins

Only three castles in Hertfordshire have left any substantial remains — at Berkhamsted, Bishop's Stortford and Hertford. In addition to these, castle earthworks survive close to the parish churches at Anstey, Great Wymondley, Pirton and Therfield, all short-lived fortifications of the Norman period. The castle remains at Benington are referred to briefly on page 74.

Berkhamsted Castle, Berkhamsted. English Heritage. Adjacent to the railway station.

In December 1066, two months after the battle of Hastings, William of Normandy arrived at Berkhamsted. To forestall an attack on London they could not withstand, the Saxons came to William at Berkhamsted and submitted. He became king and was crowned in Westminster Abbey on Christmas Day. Berkhamsted was given by William to his half-brother, Robert of Mortain. Soon afterwards work began on the earthworks of the motte and bailey (most of which still remain) and a keep and outer palisades were built. The site, originally beside an unhealthy marsh, was not well chosen, but the defences, including a double moat, were impressive. The original wooden defences were replaced in the twelfth and thirteenth centuries by stone buildings and a massive wall with circular defensive towers.

Until the end of the fifteenth century Berkhamsted was an important castle. Thomas à Becket lived here when he was Lord Chancellor. King John's queen, Isabel, was besieged here for two weeks in 1216 by the barons and a French army and the castle was captured. It is said that the earth platforms outside the north moat were built during the siege as platforms for stone-throwing mangonels, though it is doubtful whether there would have been time for this. John's son Richard later built a three-storey tower, royal apartments and a chapel.

Piers Gaveston, favourite of Edward II, owned it for a year, 1308-9. Edward, the Black Prince, imprisoned King John of France in the castle after the battle of Poitiers in 1356 and spent his own last days here. As Prince of Wales, the Black Prince was also Duke of Cornwall and from his time until 1930 the castle became part of the Duchy of Cornwall. In the absence of a Duke of Cornwall it was granted elsewhere: Catherine of Aragon, Anne Boleyn and Jane Seymour all held the honour. Queen Elizabeth I leased it in 1580 to Sir Edward Carey, who built Berkhamsted Place (now demolished) with some of the stones.

There is little masonry left today. Such remains as there are of the circular keep indicate a deep well, part of a staircase and a fireplace. The earthworks are still impressive, however. Evidence of the main entrance, which was on the south side, was destroyed when the railway was built in 1838.

Chesfield church, Graveley (OS 166: TL 247279).

The ruined church of St Etheldreda at Chesfield stands on private land, visible from the road east of Graveley. It was partly dismantled in 1750, three hundred years after Chesfield was united with the parish of Graveley. Burials continued there until 1686. Like the similarly ruined chapel at Minsden, it remains picturesque but of little antiquarian interest.

Cromer Windmill, Ardeley (OS 166: TL 304286).
Open early May to mid September, afternoons only, every Sunday and the second and fourth Wednesday in the month. Enquiries to

keyholders, telephone: 0438 861293.

The post mill stands ½ mile (800 metres) north-east of the hamlet of Cromer, on the road to Cottered. The first record of a mill here was in 1222. The present mill was built about 1800 and ceased working in about 1924. This is Hertfordshire's last surviving post mill. It was conveyed to the Hertfordshire Building Preservation Trust in 1967 and has been extensively restored during 1990/1, though not to full working order.

Digswell Viaduct (OS 166: TL 246150).

This viaduct of forty arches, designed by Lewis Cubitt, was built by Thomas Brassey in 1848-50 to carry the Great Northern Railway across the valley of the river Mimram. It is 1560 feet (475 metres) long and 100 feet (30 metres) above the river. The first train crossed on 5th August 1850. This great feat of engineering remains one of Britain's most impressive viaducts.

Hertford Castle, Hertford.

A Saxon fortified burgh is recorded on the east side of the river Lea in Hertford in AD 912. It may have provided the site for the later Norman castle, which probably originated in the time of William I. In 1141 Peter de Valognes was confirmed as governor. The gatehouse, the only substantial building remaining, was built in 1461-5. The castle, which seems often to have been in bad repair, was relinquished by the Crown to the ownership of the Earl of Salisbury in 1627. The Earl of Hillsborough, tenant in the 1790s, converted the gatehouse to a stately home: he substituted new windows, converted the archway to an entrance hall and added the three-storey extension. In 1906 Lord Salisbury offered the property to Hertford Borough Council, since when it has been used as administrative offices.

The castle grounds, now a public park, contain evidence of the original motte and bailey plan. The mound lies at the north end of the site close to the wooden bridge across the river Lea. Near it is a short length of twelfth-century curtain wall. The postern gate and polygonal tower at the south end of the gatehouse extension are also of early date. Behind them are remains of the moat. The

(Opposite) Knebworth House from the Jekyll herb garden.

Digswell Viaduct carries the London to Edinburgh railway over the Mimram valley.

Rye House Gatehouse.

main castle buildings once occupied the inner bailey on the north-east side of the gatehouse.

Minsden Chapel, Langley (OS 166: TL 199246). On a hill west of the B656 (Hitchin to Codicote) road and on the north side of the B651 to St Paul's Walden. A footpath from the Royal Oak public house which cuts across this corner to the B651 passes the site.

The origin of the ruined chapel is obscure: the earliest known reference to it was in 1487. It is believed to have remained in regular use until about 1626, and for occasional marriages until 1752. The Hitchin historian Reginald Hine (1883-1949) is buried there.

Royston Cave, Royston (OS 154: TL 357407). Telephone: 0763 242587.
Normally open in the afternoons, Saturdays, Sundays and Bank Holidays, from Easter to September.

This unique man-made chamber was discovered in 1742 beneath the south side of Melbourn Street near Royston Cross. When cleared of rubble, the bell-shaped chamber was found to be about 30 feet (9 metres) high, its walls covered by a remarkable jumble of primitive carvings depicting identifiable saints and New Testament scenes. No reliable dating evidence has been found: speculation favours the thirteenth century and a possible link with the Knights Templar, who were established near Baldock. The cave is now accessible through a marked entrance on the north side of the street.

Rye House Gatehouse, Stanstead Abbots (OS 166: TL 387099).

The fifteenth-century red-brick gatehouse stands within a rectangular moat between the river Lea and the New River, close to Rye House railway station. This gatehouse was formerly an integral part of the house which occupied the north-east quarter of the area within the moat. In 1683 Rye House was the scene of a plot to assassinate King Charles II as he passed by when returning from Newmarket to London. The plot failed and the conspirators (including Richard Rumbold, a former 'Ironside' and the then tenant of Rye House) were executed.

In 1864 the gatehouse and the nearby Rye House Hotel (formerly the King's Arms Inn, now 'Rye's') were both owned by William Henry Teale, who developed the complex as a pleasure garden in the manner of Vauxhall Gardens. It was particularly popular for firms' outings and banquets. The gatehouse is now once again part of a recreational area: the Lea Valley Regional Park. It was restored in 1970 and houses an exhibition which is open on summer weekends. Other amenities in the vicinity are an RSPB bird sanctuary (see page 53) and the Rye House motorcycle racing track.

Scott's Grotto, Scott's Road, Ware (OS 166: TL 355138). Telephone: 0920 464131.
Open Saturday and Bank Holiday afternoons, April to September. Group visits by arrangement.

Grottos (artificial caves) were fashionable garden features in the eighteenth century. This one was built by John Scott of Amwell House, probably in the 1760s. The Scotts were a Quaker family: John's father had become wealthy in the Ware malting trade, and

Hertfordshire village 'cages', or lock-ups;
(clockwise from the top) Anstey, Ashwell,
Barley, Shenley.

The castle folly at Benington Lordship Gardens.

(Opposite) Fishing on Tringford Reservoir near Tring.

Samuel, an elder brother, became prominent among Hertford Quakers. John was a minor poet, acquainted with Dr Johnson, who is said to have visited him at Amwell House. Building the grotto seems to have been a means of diverting himself, since fear of disease, which had carried off his mother and her other children, prevented him from visiting London. Amwell House has become part of the nearby Ware College, and the grotto now nestles in a picturesque hollow in Scott's Road, hemmed in by modern houses. Though small, it is elaborate in its construction. The passages, cleverly lined with flints, are decorated with patterns of shells.

Shenley Village Cage (OS 166: TL 188008).

The small beehive-shaped building in the High Street is the eighteenth-century 'cage' or lock-up, the most original in style of several which survive in Hertfordshire. It would have been used for the overnight detention of drunks and other minor malefactors due to appear before a magistrate next morning. Construction in this case is of brick. On either side of the door is the admonition: 'Be sober, Do well; Fear not, Be vigilant.' Among the Hertfordshire parishes whose cages survive in a variety of forms are Anstey, Ashwell, Barley and Layston.

Sopwell Nunnery, St Albans (OS 166: TL 152062).

The ruins known as 'Sopwell Nunnery' are not those of the medieval religious house. That was acquired by Sir Richard Lee at the Dissolution and was completely demolished. Lee built a private mansion here, no doubt reusing some old materials and retaining the monastic ground plan. His house, of which only some ruined walls remain, seems to have been abandoned soon after his death in 1575. The site beside the river Ver is evocative, though now overlooked by suburban development. There is an attractive distant view of St Albans Cathedral.

These ruins can be viewed in the course of the Ver-Colne valley walk (see page 54), which passes close by.

Temple Bar, Cheshunt (OS 166: TL 344010).

Temple Bar, designed by Sir Christopher Wren, was erected at the Fleet Street entrance to the City of London in 1672, to replace an earlier wooden structure which had been destroyed in the Great Fire of 1666. By the 1870s it was in need of repair and was also causing serious traffic congestion. It was dismantled in 1878 and acquired by Sir Henry Meux for re-erection at Theobalds Park. In spite of attempts to secure its return to the City of London it stands there to this day: neglected, vandalised, much overgrown and accessible only on foot. The four statues have been removed for restoration.

Waytemore Castle, Bishop's Stortford. Telephone: 0279 52274.

Waytemore Castle consists of an artificial mound about 42 feet (13 metres) high beside the river Stort, now surrounded by a recreation area. The bailey lay to the south. On the summit are remains of a rectangular flint structure, probably of the twelfth century, but very little survives above ground level. This castle is assumed to be one of those erected by William the Conqueror, though it may possibly have been Saxon in origin, associated with Edward the Elder's action against the Danes in AD 913. Its importance derives from its commanding position above the ford over the river Stort. The Stortford estate had been purchased by the Bishop of London shortly before the Conquest (hence the name Bishop's Stortford) and remained in the possession of the see until 1868. The castle site is now the property of the East Herts District Council. Access to the summit is normally kept locked.

8
Museums

Ashwell

Ashwell Village Museum, Swan Street, Ashwell SG7 5NY. Telephone: 0462 742155.
Open Sunday and Bank Holiday afternoons.

This remarkable museum began as the private collection of two schoolboys, Albert Sheldrick and John Bray. It was first displayed in a garden shed in 1927. Two years later, with enthusiastic support from local people, the present building was purchased in a derelict state and renovated. It had been built early in the sixteenth century, possibly as the Abbot of Westminster's office for the collection of tithes. Later it became known as the Town House and served many other purposes. In the 1830s it is known to have been a tailor's shop.

The museum was opened here on 29th November 1930; its accommodation was much extended in 1983. The collection illustrates the natural history, archaeology and social history of Ashwell and its neighbourhood from earliest times. Agricultural, trade and domestic 'bygones' have a major place. Strong links with the community are assured by a vigorous body of 'Friends of Ashwell Museum'.

Bishop's Stortford

Bishop's Stortford Local History Museum, Cemetery Lodge, Apton Road, Bishop's Stortford. Telephone: 0279 722557.
Open May to September. Telephone for details.

This is a small museum, opened in 1979, run by the Bishop's Stortford and District Local History Society with support from the town council. The building (1855), designed by local architect G. E. Pritchett, was originally the house of the cemetery foreman. Photographs, documents, archaeological finds and bygones all illustrate aspects of the past life of the area. The museum has a small reserve collection, from which temporary exhibitions are assembled on selected themes, and now houses the Sir Walter Gilbey archive.

Rhodes Memorial Museum and Commonwealth Centre, South Road, Bishop's Stortford CM23 3JG. Telephone: 0279 651746.
Open Tuesday to Saturday.

Cecil Rhodes (1853-1902) was born in this house. It was then called Netteswell House, the home of his father, the vicar of Bishop's Stortford. Cecil went to Africa at the age of seventeen and made his life there. The museum records his life but provides also a brief background to his early years in Bishop's Stortford. This house and the house adjoining were purchased as a memorial in 1938. Since 1963 the building has provided certain recreational facilities which are available to local organisations.

Chipping Barnet

Barnet Museum, 31 Wood Street, Chipping Barnet EN5 4BE. Telephone: 081-440 8066.
Open Tuesday, Wednesday and Thursday afternoons, Saturday mornings and afternoons.

This museum is run by the Barnet and District Local History Society with the support of the London Borough of Barnet. Local prints, photographs and bygones predominate. There are also sections devoted to costume and to archaeological excavations in the area. Special displays include the Barnet Fire Service, clay pipes, a Victorian room, scientific instruments made in Barnet between 1906 and 1981 by Watson Microscopes, and copies of heraldic devices relating to the battle of Barnet.

Great Amwell

Museum of Street Lighting (Concrete Utilities Ltd), Great Amwell, Ware. Telephone: 0920 462272.
Open by appointment only.

This is a collection of some 150 lighting columns and related equipment, collected and maintained by a firm engaged in their present-day provision. Painted cast-iron heraldic panels formerly used by some lighting authorities

Scott's Grotto at Ware.

(Opposite) Cromer postmill is the county's best preserved windmill.

The New River at Great Amwell.

('Board of Works, Poplar District'; 'Vestry of the Parish of Lambeth, 1856') are among the nostalgic attractions.

Harpenden
Harpenden Local History Centre, Harpenden Hall, Harpenden. Telephone: 0582 712998.
Open on the first Saturday in each month.
The local history society's museum has a small permanent collection. Each month material on a previously announced theme is displayed. Materials collected from society members and from the community are assembled, annotated and exhibited as a group activity by members. The centre is also open, by appointment only, for research purposes.

Harpenden Railway Museum, 235 Luton Road, Harpenden AL5 3DE. Telephone: 0582 713524.
Open to visitors on a few days each year.

'The Samaritan Woman' in the garden of Lowewood Museum, Hoddesdon.

This is a private museum, assembled by Geoff and Sue Woodward in their own house and garden. The collection of railwayana, started in 1963, contains several thousand items, many of them originating in Hertfordshire. Their interest in showing what they have collected is infectious, and it is not necessary to be a fellow enthusiast to enjoy a visit.

Hatfield
Mill Green Museum and Mill, Hatfield AL9 5PD. Telephone: 0707 271362.
Open daily.
Administered by the Welwyn Hatfield District Council, this museum is situated between Hatfield and Welwyn Garden City, just north of the A414/A100(intersection. Displays illustrate archaeology and local history in the area. Craft demonstrations and other special events are often arranged at summer weekends. The museum occupies the former miller's house, adjoining the watermill. There is little doubt that this was one of the four mills in Hatfield mentioned in Domesday Book.

The present building probably dates mainly from 1762, with further major alterations in 1824. The mill ceased operating commercially in 1911, when the tenant, Sydney Christmas Lawrance, emigrated to Australia. There followed a period of neglect and decay, during which some of the machinery was dismantled. The mill has now been restored to working order and is in part-time use and open to visitors. Freshly ground flour can be purchased.

Hertford
Hertford Museum, Bull Plain, Hertford SG14 1DT. Telephone: 0992 582686.
Open Tuesday to Saturday.
This museum forms a major source of information about the geology, natural environment, archaeology and history of the whole of east Hertfordshire. Displays illustrate all these aspects of the locality, including in particular agriculture, local industries and the Hertfordshire Regiment. There are extensive research collections of printed records, prints and drawings and photographs. The museum also holds the research library of the East Herts Archaeological Society.

The First Garden City Museum at Letchworth.

Hitchin

Hitchin Museum and Art Gallery, Paynes Park, Hitchin SG5 1EQ. Telephone: 0462 434476.

Open daily except Bank Holidays: afternoons only on Sundays.

Displays on the history of the area are supported by extensive research collections, local trades being particularly well represented. There is a gallery devoted to the museum's collection of nineteenth- and twentieth-century costume, the largest in the county, and a room housing artefacts from the Hertfordshire Yeomanry and Artillery Trust. A Victorian chemist's shop from the High Street has been reconstructed in the museum, complete with its stock and fittings. Outside, it is complemented by an attractive 'physic garden' containing more than a hundred herbs used for medicinal or household purposes. The art gallery presents a regularly changing programme of art and craft exhibitions, often accompanied by demonstrations and workshops. A students' room is available for visitors wishing to consult the museum's rich collections of local photographs, maps and documentary material.

Hoddesdon

Lowewood Museum, High Street, Hoddesdon EN11 8BH. Telephone: 0992 445596.

Open Tuesday to Saturday.

Lowewood, a Georgian building of about 1750, contains a museum which reflects the archaeology and local history of the whole of the borough of Broxbourne, which includes Hoddesdon, Cheshunt and Waltham Cross. One room is devoted to a series of temporary exhibitions. Research materials include an impressive collection of photographs.

Near the museum stands the statue known as 'The Samaritan Woman'. From 1631 to 1826 it stood in the market place at Hoddesdon as the conduit head for the supply of fresh water which was brought to the town by Sir Marmaduke Rawdon.

Letchworth

First Garden City Heritage Museum, 296 Norton Way South, Letchworth SG6 1SU. Telephone: 0462 683149.

Open Monday to Friday afternoons, Saturday mornings and afternoons. Closed Sundays, Christmas Day and Boxing Day.

King James I's hunting lodge at Royston.

(Opposite) The Mill Green Museum and Mill near Hatfield.

The Victorian cottage garden and the bee shelter at the Forge Museum in Much Hadham.

The museum collects and displays material on the Garden City Movement and the development of Letchworth since its selection as the site of the first garden city in 1903. Inevitably it reflects the wider social history of the twentieth century as well as that of Letchworth itself. The museum occupies the former drawing office (1907) of architects Barry Parker and Raymond Unwin, key figures in the design and development of Letchworth. Barry Parker's office is preserved as it was in his day and there is an extensive collection of material relating to his architectural work generally.

Letchworth Museum and Art Gallery, Broadway, Letchworth SG6 3PF. Telephone: 0462 685647.
Open daily except Sundays and Bank Holidays.
This centrally situated museum contains exhibits on local geology and natural history and an extensive archaeological collection, for which this is the main research centre in a wide area of north Hertfordshire. There is also an art gallery with changing exhibitions.

Standalone Farm Centre, Wilbury Road, Letchworth SG6 4JN. Telephone: 0462 686775.
Open daily, March to September.
This long-established working farm, preserved as a living museum for the benefit of the community, is open both to school parties and to the general public. In addition to its animals, crops and demonstrations of milking and the work of the blacksmith, the farm has a collection of old farm machinery. One area has been developed for the observation of wildfowl. A shop, refreshment room and picnic area are available, and special facilities are provided for teachers and schools.

Much Hadham
The Forge Museum and Victorian Cottage Garden, High Street, Much Hadham SG10 6BS (opposite the village hall). Telephone: 0279 843301.
Open at weekends, and on some weekdays during the summer. Telephone for details.
This forge was worked by four generations of the Page family of blacksmiths from 1811, when Frederick brought his bride to Much

Hadham, until 1980. Charles Page, Frederick's great-grandson, died in 1983 at the age of 91. The Forge Museum contains a collection of the tools and materials used here, and objects made or repaired by the blacksmith. There are temporary exhibitions and demonstrations of shoeing and other crafts. A blacksmith is again working commercially on the premises. The cottage garden contains an early nineteenth-century bee shelter. The forge and its contents have been restored by the Hertfordshire Building Preservation Trust.

Royston

Royston Museum, Lower King Street, Royston SG4 7AL. Telephone: 0763 242587.
Open Wednesdays, Thursdays and Saturdays, and on summer Sunday afternoons and Bank Holiday Mondays.

The museum occupies the former building of the Congregational Schoolroom (1879-1981). Its collection deals mainly with Royston's changing scene and social life; there is an archaeological gallery and a growing index of local historical information is available to researchers. There are special exhibitions each month, and frequent exhibitions from other sources. The museum is managed by the Royston Town Council in conjunction with the Royston and District Local History Society.

St Albans

Kingsbury Watermill Museum, St Michael's Street, St Albans AL3 4SJ. Telephone: 0727 53502.
Open daily except Mondays, afternoons only on Sundays.

Kingsbury was an ancient Saxon royal manor, ownership of which passed to the abbots of St Albans and after the Dissolution to Sir Nicholas Bacon's Gorhambury estate. The mill is situated on the river Ver in the village of St Michael's. The present building is mainly of the sixteenth century, with an eighteenth-century façade. Milling machinery is well displayed and explained. The building incorporates a collection of agricultural implements, a craft shop and a restaurant.

The Museum of St Albans, Hatfield Road, St Albans. Telephone: 0727 819340.
Open daily, afternoons only on Sunday.

The Museum of St Albans is concerned with natural history and with the medieval and later history of St Albans. It has the

Kingsbury Watermill Museum, St Albans, and (right) Royston Museum.

The scallop shell mosaic in Verulamium Museum, St Albans.

(Opposite) The Village Museum at Ashwell.

A statuette of Venus in Verulamium Museum, St Albans.

important Salaman Collection of craft tools, redisplayed in a new gallery. There are an urban wildlife garden and a special exhibitions gallery.

St Albans Organ Museum, 320 Camp Road (next to Camp School), St Albans. Telephone: 0727 51557.
Open Sunday afternoons, except Christmas Day.

Originally the private collection of the late Mr Charles Hart, this museum is administered by the St Albans Musical Museum Society. It is accommodated in a large auditorium, all at ground-floor level. The decor is reminiscent of a 1930s cinema, and the splendour of the great instruments is complemented by the friendly enthusiasm of the society members who staff the museum and demonstrate the exhibits on Sunday afternoons, the programme running from 2.15 to 4.30. The collection includes Mortier, DeCap and Bursens mechanical organs, Rutt and Wurlitzer theatre organs and many other mechanical instruments and musical boxes.

Verulamium Museum, St Michael's, St Albans AL3 4SW. Telephone: 0727 819339; schools bookings and information service: 0727 819341.
Open daily, afternoons only on Sundays.

On the site of one of Roman Britain's major cities, Verulamium Museum was

The Walter Rothschild Museum at Tring.

opened in 1934 and today is one of the main centres for the appreciation of everyday life in Roman Britain. Completely redisplayed in 1992, the museum exhibits mosaic floors, painted wall plaster, glass, ceramics and personal possessions, presented with the aid of re-created Roman rooms, excavation videos, hands-on features, accessible storage and touch-screen computers.

Shenley

The Mosquito Aircraft Museum, Salisbury Hall, London Colney, near St Albans. Telephone: 0727 822051.

Open March to October, Saturdays, Sundays and Bank Holidays; also on Thursday afternoons.

This museum, run by the De Havilland Aircraft Museum Trust Ltd, is situated on the B556 one mile (1.6 km) south of London Colney, 1/2 mile (800 metres) from Junction 22 on the M25. The first Mosquito aircraft was built here in 1940 and transported to the De Havilland airfield at Hatfield by road. Manufacture continued here until 1944. The museum now houses the prototype Mosquito of 1940 and a collection of sixteen other De Havilland aircraft together with a variety of

engines and an extensive display of aeronautical memorabilia. It serves as an information and documentation centre for enthusiasts. (Salisbury Hall itself is not open to the public.)

Stevenage

Stevenage Museum, St George's Way, Stevenage SG1 1XX. Telephone: 0438 354292.

Open Monday to Saturday, except Bank Holidays.

The museum occupies the undercroft of St George's church. Its displays tell in a most attractive way the story of life in Stevenage from earliest times to the present. There is also a programme of changing exhibitions. The museum has published a variety of pamphlets on aspects of the history of the area.

Tring

Walter Rothschild Zoological Museum, Akeman Street, Tring HP23 6AP. Telephone: 0442 824181.

Open daily; afternoons only on Sundays; closed Good Friday, 24th to 26th December, and 1st January.

Originally the private collection of the sec-

Watford Museum, formerly part of Benskins brewery.

ond Baron Rothschild, this museum was given to the nation in 1937 and became an annexe to the Natural History Museum. The galleries, built in the 1890s, retain their original character in spite of considerable modernisation in 1972. The collection contains specimens of a thousand species of mammal, as well as hundreds of different birds, reptiles, fishes and insects. Their magnificence and variety is awesome. They include rare, endangered, bizarre and beautiful species, from dressed fleas to extinct giant sloths.

Ware

Ware Museum, Priory Lodge, High Street, Ware SG12 9AL. Telephone: 0920 487848. *Open Saturdays and Sunday afternoons.*

This museum consists of a permanent exhibition on the history of Ware, together with changing displays on topics relating to Ware.

Watford

Watford Museum, 194 High Street, Watford WD1 2HG. Telephone: 0923 232297.

Open Monday to Saturday, including Bank Holidays.

The museum occupies a handsome mansion built as a private residence in 1775. This became associated with the Cannon Brewery, which was taken over by Benskins in 1867, and the house was eventually used as the offices of the company. The brewery vacated the premises in 1977 and it was converted for use as the town's museum. Collections already existed consisting mainly of local history materials and fine arts, and these have become the main themes of the museum.

Brewing, because of its links with the site, and printing, Watford's major industry during the twentieth century, have become other primary areas of interest. To these have been added transport and the general social history of the area, and there is a special display on Watford Football Club. There is also an art gallery. In its first year the museum won an award in the 'Museum of the Year' competition.

9
Famous people

Few of Hertfordshire's eminent former residents or visitors can be clearly associated with particular buildings or locations which we can still see today. The **Cecil** family at Hatfield and the novelist **Bulwer-Lytton** at Knebworth still speak to us through their houses (pages 75 and 76) which are of wider interest in themselves; the home of **Francis Bacon** is a ruin in the grounds of Gorhambury House (see page 75) and the birthplace of **Cecil Rhodes** at Bishop's Stortford is a museum (see page 87).

Two eminent churchmen spent their formative years in the county: **Nicholas Breakspear**, the only English Pope (crowned Adrian IV in 1154), was born at Bedmond in Abbots Langley; and **Thomas à Becket**, the Archbishop of Canterbury martyred in 1170, received as his first benefice the parish of Bramfield. But no trace remains of their passing; the present parish church at Bramfield dates mainly from 1840.

Anthony Trollope spent eleven productive years at Waltham Cross, but his house does not survive, and the homes of the novelist **Mrs Humphrey Ward** (Stocks, Aldbury, now a hotel) and of the grandfather of **Beatrix Potter**, where she spent such happy times in her childhood (Campfield Place, Essendon, now a private house), remain remote within their enclosures. There are just a few places, however, where we can feel very close to some famous people of the past.

Sir Henry Bessemer (1813-98)

The parents of Henry Bessemer moved from Paris to Charlton, near Hitchin, at the time of the French Revolution. Eight years later their son Henry was born in what is now known as Charlton House, opposite the Windmill public house. A plaque on the wall records the event. Bessemer senior, who had been a typefounder in Paris, continued that work in association with Henry Caslon, who was to be young Henry's godfather. Henry Bessemer's autobiography records that he obtained his first experience of working with metal in his father's workshop here, while his fascination with machinery was stimulated by the many hours he spent studying the working of the flour mill at the other end of the village.

After the family moved to London in 1830 Henry entered upon a lifetime of research, mainly in the field of metallurgy. His most important achievement was the discovery of an improved method of making steel from crude iron by passing air through the molten metal. Increased prosperity enabled him to move from St Pancras to a new home at Highgate which he called Charlton House. There, as his autobiography records, 'I could sometimes ... almost fancy myself at my dear old birthplace, Charlton, and myself again a village boy.'

George Chapman (about 1559-1634)

Chapman, eminent poet and playwright and a contemporary of Shakespeare, is best remembered for his translations of Homer, most of all because they inspired one of Keats's greatest sonnets, 'On first looking into Chapman's Homer'. Two references link Chapman with Hitchin: his father's will, proved in 1589, describes him as 'of Hytchin in the countye of Hertford'; and his own first poem, 'Euthymiae Raptus' (1609) refers to his 'native air ... on the hill next Hitchin's left hand'. That could certainly be understood to describe Tilehouse Street, but the identification of Western House, 35 Tilehouse Street (now largely rebuilt but marked with a plaque), as his birthplace and ancestral home rests largely on local tradition.

Charles Dickens (1812-70)

Dickens was still a newspaper reporter for the *Morning Chronicle* when he made his first known visit to Hertfordshire in November 1835. He came to Hatfield to report on the dramatic fire at Hatfield House which resulted in the death of the 85-year-old Dowager Lady Salisbury and destroyed much of the west wing of the house. During this short visit Dickens must have become familiar with Fore Street, which leads down the hill from the main gate of the house, and with the Eight Bells public house at its foot.

No doubt too he was already drafting *Oliver Twist*, which began publication just over a year later. In that novel there occurs the murder of Nancy by Bill Sikes, who then made for Hatfield. He entered the town by the London road, went down Fore Street and entered a small public house, undoubtedly the Eight Bells. Dickens describes the scene in the tap room, local people drinking by the fire, and the entry of a pedlar who noticed the bloodstains on Sikes's hat. The interior has been much altered since Dickens's day. Two of Dickens's later short stories, 'Mrs Lirriper's Lodgings' and 'Mrs Lirriper's Legacy', also described Fore Street and particularly the Salisbury Arms, the coaching inn at the top end of the street where Dickens perhaps stayed either in 1835 or on a later visit. The building survives, but it is no longer an inn.

In later life Dickens became a close friend of Sir Edward Bulwer-Lytton of Knebworth (see page 76). In 1850 he brought a company of eminent amateur actors to perform in the great hall of Knebworth House, himself serving as stage manager as well as taking part in the performances. The success of this venture prompted Dickens and Bulwer-Lytton to conceive the idea of financing a charity by such performances, in order to establish a 'Guild of Literature and Art'. The main object was to provide a home for 'needy and aged actors and artists'. This also seemed to be successful, and in 1865 a house was opened on the London Road south of old Stevenage High Street, not far from Knebworth House and close to the site of the present Stevenage Leisure Centre. Unfortunately the scheme ultimately failed because the intended beneficiaries declined to move out from London. The house was demolished in the early 1960s.

E. M. Forster (1879-1970)

The novelist E. M. Forster lived at Rooks Nest House, Stevenage, with his widowed mother from the age of four until he was fourteen, when they moved to Tonbridge. The house, so far untouched by the growth of Stevenage New Town, remains in private occupation. It is situated just north of Rooks Nest Farm, beside the lane which passes eastward in front of the parish church (see page 72) in the direction of Weston (OS 166: TL 244267). Forster's novel *Howards End*, published in 1910, draws particularly on his recollections of Stevenage. The house, Howards End, is Rooks Nest House; the village referred to as Hilton is a somewhat adapted Stevenage. Forster's affection for the town did not fade. In *Two Cheers for Democracy* (1951) he wrote: 'I was brought up as a boy in one of the home counties, in a district which I still think the loveliest in England. There is nothing special about it — it is agricultural land, and could not be described in terms of beauty spots. It must always have looked much the same. I have kept in touch with it, going back to it as an abiding city and still visiting the house which was once my home, for it is occupied by friends.'

Lady Caroline Lamb (1785-1827)

Brocket Hall and Park are situated to the west of Welwyn Garden City and the village of Lemsford. The house, now a conference centre, can be seen from a public footpath which crosses the park: from a stile near the mill in Lemsford village to another at a lay-by on the north side of the A6129 road between Stanborough and Wheathampstead. The house was the family home of William Lamb, Lord Melbourne, Queen Victoria's first prime minister, but it will always be associated with his wife, Caroline.

The house, rather austere in its external appearance, was built for an earlier Lamb in the 1760s. The first meeting between William and Caroline took place when she attended a

Button Snap near Westmill, once owned by Charles Lamb.

party here as a very young girl. They did not marry until 1805, when she came immediately to Brocket, which she always loved, though she was to spend much of her time in London. The marriage, never easy, eventually broke down following her disastrous liaison with Lord Byron and the mental illness which it precipitated. It is said that one day in 1824 she was out riding near Brocket Hall when she came face to face with Byron's funeral cortege making its slow way towards Nottingham. Although it seems unlikely that this encounter was entirely fortuitous, the experience brought on a complete nervous collapse. Caroline and William legally separated in the following year.

Caroline expressed her great distress at the need to leave her beloved Brocket in a touching poem:

'An exile from these scenes I go,
Whither I neither care nor know;
Perhaps to some far distant shore,
Never again to know you more.
The river Lea glides smoothly by,
Unconscious of my agony.'

She died in London in 1827 and was buried in Hatfield church.

Charles Lamb (1775-1834)

The essayist Charles Lamb (unrelated to the Lambs of Brocket Hall) had a deep affection for this county. As a small child he had spent happy holidays with his great-aunt at Mackery End Farm (near the house of that name north-east of Harpenden), and also at Blakesware (near Widford), where his grandmother was housekeeper. (She was virtually mistress of the house, since the owners, the Plumer family, did not occupy it during the years when Charles knew it.) His grandmother died in 1792 when he was seventeen.

In 1809 Charles's godfather Francis Field died leaving most of his property to his wife Sarah. It included the small cottage in Westmill now known as Button Snap, perhaps Charles's own whimsical name for it, which Sarah conveyed to him three years later. It was, and is, in an isolated spot (OS 166: TL 349265) nearly 4 miles (6 km) walk from Puckeridge, where he would probably have alighted from the London coach. His joy in its possession is recorded in the essay 'My First Play': 'When I journeyed down to take possession, and planted foot on my own ground ... I strode with larger paces over my

McAdam House in Hoddesdon.

allotment of three-quarters of an acre ... with the feeling of an English freeholder that all betwixt sky and centre was my own.'

There is no evidence that Lamb ever lived at Button Snap: with an office to attend in London he would scarcely have found that convenient. We know that only three years later it was occupied by a tenant, Mr Sargus, when in February 1815 Charles Lamb conveyed it to Thomas Greg of Coles Park, Westmill. The cottage is still a private residence, but marked by a tasteful plaque on the turf outside.

David Livingstone (1813-73)

For a short period of nine months in 1857 the missionary-explorer David Livingstone lived with his wife and four children in Monken Hadley, in a house facing Hadley Green. He had been in Africa since 1840 and

this was his first period of leave, during which he wrote his book *Missionary Travels and Researches in South Africa*. Although he found writing a drudgery, he recorded that 'we spent no pleasanter time in England than the months in Hadley'. The house, now known as Livingstone Cottage, bears a handsome plaque which is visible from the main road. A later resident here was James Agate, the eminent drama critic.

John Loudon McAdam (1756-1836)

McAdam, a native of Ayrshire, became the outstanding road engineer of his day, when increasing heavy traffic was making the improvement of roads a matter of great urgency. He and his sons were appointed surveyors to many of the turnpike trusts, with immense benefit to the roads for which they were responsible. In 1827, when McAdam was 71, he married as his second wife, against strong opposition from his family, Anne Charlotte Delancy, aged forty. They made their home in Hoddesdon, in a house in the High Street which is now occupied by Lloyd's Bank. The last ten years of his life seem to have passed happily here. He made an annual visit to Scotland and died there in the autumn of 1836. He is buried in Moffat churchyard. A plaque was placed on the Hoddesdon house in 1936, the centenary of his death, and there is a memorial in Broxbourne church.

Henry Moore (1898-1986)

In 1941, when his London studio was damaged by bombing, the eminent sculptor Henry Moore made his home and established new studios at Perry Green, near Much Hadham. He was to continue living there until his death in 1986, enlarging the property and developing a parklike landscape in which his sculptures could be shown to advantage. He greatly loved the peaceful countryside and defended it strongly in 1982 when it was threatened by the extension of Stansted Airport: 'It is perhaps not too fanciful to think that the many hundreds of my bronzes sold since 1941 have exported a bit of the peace of this corner of Hertfordshire to the many cities, at home and abroad, where they now stand.'

The Henry Moore Foundation, based at Perry Green, was established in 1977 to promote interest in sculpture, endow scholarships and subsidise exhibitions. Opportunities to visit the Foundation properties are very limited. Conducted tours are provided on certain afternoons during the summer months, strictly by appointment only. Applications should be made in writing, well in advance, to The Henry Moore Foundation, Dane Tree House, Perry Green, Much Hadham, Hertfordshire SG10 6EE.

George Orwell (1903-50)

In April 1936 George Orwell (Eric Blair) moved into the small white cottage (given a large rear-ward extension in the 1980s) next to the Plough public house in the village of

George Orwell's cottage in Wallington.

Wallington, near Baldock. The cottage had been found for him by friends: he had no previous connection with the area. Five weeks after moving in he married his first wife, Eileen O'Shaughnessy, in the parish church (see page 72).

He had come for peace and quiet in which to write *The Road to Wigan Pier*, but he also needed to supplement his income. The cottage had formerly been the village shop and he continued to run it as such, in the afternoons only. The book was finished on 15th December, and a few days later he left for Barcelona and the Spanish Civil War. He was discharged on medical grounds and returned to Wallington in the following July. Until February 1938 he worked in his cottage on *Homage to Catalonia*. A tubercular infection then obliged him to enter hospital for some time and subsequently to spend the winter in a warm climate: he and Eileen went to Morocco.

When the Blairs returned in the spring of 1939 Eric's main concern was with the wildlife around the cottage. The pond up by the church had become stagnant and covered with slime, but he was glad to find there were still a few newts in it. He remained at Wallington till May 1940, when the couple found a tenant for the cottage and moved to a flat near Regent's Park. Five years later he published *Animal Farm*, set in the fictitious 'Manor Farm, Willingdon'. Manor Farm, Wallington, had been just a few steps from his front door. The cottage is still a private residence.

George Bernard Shaw (1856-1950)

Shaw came to live at the New Rectory (renamed 'Shaw's Corner'), Ayot St Lawrence, in 1906 and stayed there until his death in 1950. The house is now a National Trust property and is open to the public (see page 78). It is reliably recorded that he had found in the churchyard a gravestone inscribed: 'Mary Anne South. Born 1825. Died 1895. Her time was short.' Thinking this a good testimonial to the village, he promptly acquired the so-called 'New Rectory' and moved in.

He was already fifty years old, with an enormous reputation and a formidable catalogue of achievements. Later works undertaken at Ayot St Lawrence included *Pygmalion* and *St Joan*. Shaw's study, with his papers and personal belongings left just as in his lifetime, is now open to view, together with the kitchen and pantry, and the wooden summerhouse in the garden, a favourite working place.

In spite of his prickly reputation, Shaw developed a great affection for Ayot St Lawrence. His last completed work was a *Rhyming Picture Guide* to the village, his own doggerel verses illustrated by his own photographs making a wonderful farewell tribute:

This is my dell, and this my dwelling
Their charm so far beyond my telling
That though in Ireland is my birthplace
This house shall be my final earthplace.

His ashes were scattered in the garden.

10
Tourist information centres

Berkhamsted: Berkhamsted Library, Kings Road, Berkhamsted HP4 3BD. Telephone: 0442 864545.

Bishop's Stortford: 2 The Causeway, Bishop's Stortford CM22 2EJ. Telephone: 0279 655261 extension 251.

Borehamwood: Civic Offices, Elstree Way, Borehamwood WD6 1WA. Telephone: 081-207 2277.

Hemel Hempstead: Pavilion Box Office, Marlowes, Hemel Hempstead HP1 1HA. Telephone: 0442 64451.

Hertford: The Castle, Hertford SG14 1HR. Telephone: 0992 584322.

Hitchin: Hitchin Library, Paynes Park, Hitchin SG5 1EW. Telephone: 0462 434738 or 450133.

Rickmansworth: 46 High Street, Rickmansworth WD3 1HJ. Telephone: 0923 776611.

St Albans: Town Hall, Market Place, St Albans AL3 5DJ. Telephone: 0727 864511.

South Mimms: M25 Motorway Services, South Mimms, Potters Bar EN6 3QQ. Telephone: 0707 43233.

Stevenage: Central Library, Southgate, Stevenage SG1 1HD. Telephone: 0438 369441.

Welwyn Garden City: Campus West, The Campus, Welwyn Garden City AL8 6BX. Telephone: 0707 332880.

11
Further reading

Most of the towns and many of the parishes of Hertfordshire have their own local histories which provide detailed information about their localities. A selection of the more recent of these local histories is included in this list, which is otherwise concerned with the county as a whole.

Ashby, Margaret. *Forster Country*. Flaunden Press, 1991.

Ballin, Frank, and Tomkins, Malcolm. *Hertfordshire Yesterdays*. Kylin Press, 1982.

Beachcroft, T. O., and Emms, W. B. *Five Hide Village: a History of Datchworth*. Datchworth Parish Council, 1984.

Branigan, Keith. *Town and Country: the Archaeology of Verulamium and the Roman Chilterns*. Spurbooks, 1973.

Cecil, David. *The Cecils of Hatfield House*. Constable, 1973.

Chauncy, Sir Henry. *The Historical Antiquities of Hertfordshire*. 1700.

Clutterbuck, Robert. *The History and Antiquities of the County of Hertford*. Three volumes, 1815-27.

Cussans, J. E. *History of Hertfordshire*. Stephen Austin, 1870-81 (reprinted as three volumes by EP Publishing Ltd, 1972).

Timber frame and thatch at Barkway.

Davis, K. Rutherford. *Britons and Saxons: the Chiltern Region, 400-700.* Phillimore, 1982.

Farris, Noël. *The Wymondleys.* Hertfordshire Publications, 1989.

Garden Cities and New Towns. Hertfordshire Publications, 1990.

Gover, J. E. B., and others. *The Place-names of Hertfordshire.* Cambridge University Press, 1970.

Hastie, Scott. *Kings Langley: a Hertfordshire Village.* Kings Langley Local History and Museum Society, 1991.

Johnson, W. Branch. *The Industrial Archaeology of Hertfordshire.* David & Charles, 1970.

Johnson, W. Branch (editor). *'Memorandums for ...': the Diary between 1798 and 1810 of John Carrington.* Phillimore, 1973.

Jones-Baker, Doris. *Old Hertfordshire Calendar.* Phillimore, 1974.

Jones-Baker, Doris (editor). *Hertfordshire in History.* Hertfordshire Local History Council, 1991.

Maddren, Maureen (editor). *Baldock Voices: the Town as Remembered by Baldock People.* Egon Publishers, 1991.

Miller, Mervyn. *Letchworth: the First Garden City.* Phillimore, 1989.

Munby, Lionel. *The Hertfordshire Landscape.* Hodder & Stoughton, 1977.

Poole, Helen, and Fleck, Alan (editors). *Old Hitchin: Portrait of an English Market Town.* Eric Moore and North Hertfordshire Museums, 1976.

Robinson, Gwennah. *Hertfordshire* (Barracuda 'Guide to County History' series). Barracuda Books, 1978.

Rook, Tony. *A History of Hertfordshire.* Phillimore, 1984.

Sawford, Brian. *Wild Flower Habitats of Hertfordshire: Past, Present and Future?* Castlemead Publications, Ware, 1990.

Sheldrick, Albert. *A Different World: Ashwell before 1939.* Cortney Publications, 1991.

Sheldrick, Gillian. *The Hart Reguardant: Hertfordshire County Council 1889-1989.* Hertfordshire Publications, 1989.

Victoria History of England: Hertfordshire. Four volumes and index, A. Constable, 1902-14.

Wayne, Joan (editor). *A Foot on Three Daisies: Pirton's Story.* Pirton Local History Group, 1987.

Whitmore, Richard. *Victorian and Edwardian Hertfordshire from Old Photographs.* Batsford, 1976.

Index